Family on the Loose

The Art of Traveling with Kids

Family
on the
Loose

The Art of
Traveling with Kids

Bill Richards and E. Ashley Steel

Rumble Books
Bellevue, Washington

Published by Rumble Books
Bellevue, Washington 98007
info@rumblebooks.com

First Edition: November 2012

Library of Congress Control Number (LCCN) 2012916923

ISBN 978-0615696539 (Rumble Books)

Printed in the United States of America

For our grandchildren and our great grandchildren...

Contents

Introduction

Experience, travel—these are an education in themselves.
—Euripides, circa 450 B.C.

This book is here to tell you and your family to pack your bags, hop a plane, and take a trip! Family travel is an exciting adventure that opens up new worlds of customs, tastes, architecture, art, politics, religions, ideas, and more. Travelers discover that the everyday basics of life are open to infinite variety. Some people eat dinner at ten in the evening, some eat rice for breakfast, and some stop at a moment's notice to pray in the street. We are never too young (or too old!) to learn that there is rarely only one right way to do something or to remember that people around the world share the same basic human needs and emotions.

Embarking on a journey with your kids can be more rewarding than any traveling you have done before. It's a new adventure for everyone. Kids will be energetic, inquisitive, excited, and surprisingly brave. They will open up cultural doors for you as strangers ask them questions, storekeepers speak to them in broken English, and local children invite them to play at the park. As in other aspects of your life, kids will shed new light on things you might otherwise see through the dulled lens of adult experience. Their energy will be contagious! But children will also be timid, unsure, exhausted, and homesick at times. They will need to know what to expect in the next five minutes, five hours, and five days.

In addition to being fun, traveling is also a great opportunity for developing skills that your kids will find useful back home—and they won't even know it's part of their education. Basics like geography, economics, math, biology, and writing can become part of the adventure. Sometimes at home it's hard to find the time to go over multiplication tables yet again. But converting prices to your home currency, getting correct change when buying a souvenir, and budgeting spending money all demand math skills. Kids won't be able to avoid their math facts and will never again wonder "When will I ever need to know this stuff?" Ecology, art history, political science, and more, can be deeply explored on a family adventure. Who doesn't become immersed in history while traveling through Europe? Or become fascinated by comparative religion while traveling through Asia? Classroom learning and reading books are great ways to learn facts, but there is no substitute for first-hand experience. On the road, your kids will discover that learning is part of living.

Travel is also a fabulous way to develop your family's unique set of shared values. As you explore other cultures and compare them to home, you will all learn more about yourselves and about each other. Insights and ideas will emerge in a multitude of ways: conversations in the café, people-watching on the train, and writing in journals. Maybe your family will find a new holiday or family tradition to share for years to come. Perhaps your family will decide to raise money for an overseas charity. Observing how religion infuses culture with beliefs, symbols, and ideas will spark conversations about your own family's religion and beliefs. You will collectively develop new ways of being in the world, and perhaps make new commitments to each other and to the communities you inhabit. At a bare minimum, you will be rewarded with a mountain of family memories and stories.

As parents, we strive to give our kids the best possible childhood and upbringing. We enrich and support our kids through homework help and after-school activities. We join the PTA, monitor screen time, and buy books. But even the most nurturing family life can suffer from the monotony of carpool schedules and homework nagging, the doldrums of suburban chores, and the constant refrain, "I'm gonna count to three..." Travel will be good for you and good for the kids. It will be great for all of you to leap into another culture, challenge yourselves, and learn firsthand about the world together.

This book is packed with easy-to-use ideas to make your trip a successful adventure. In the first section, we help you plan and prepare for your trip in an engaging and exciting way. Preparation ahead of time is the key to a rewarding journey. The second section of the book is devoted to the trip itself, with suggestions that will make the experience easier and more enjoyable for everyone. In the third and final section of the book, we help bring the adventure home, an often-forgotten but essential part of the travel experience. We explain the basics in the main text but, knowing how limited reading time can be for parents, we've also condensed a vast amount of additional information into quickly browsable "travel tips" and lists.

Wait, wait. There's more! We also have a website, familyontheloose.com, where you can find extended travel anecdotes, new tips and education ideas, destination-specific advice, bargain travel tips, and some random philosophical musings. Regular updates include new posts and readers' comments, questions, and feedback. We're particularly interested in what did and didn't work for different families and in new twists readers devise on our approach.

This book is intended for both well-seasoned travelers and newbies alike who enjoy being with their children and are excited to discover (or rediscover) the vast and unique experiences this world has to offer. By encouraging parents and children to travel together, we hope to help you foster a new generation of individuals who are tolerant, respectful of cultural differences, and ready to lead a new global society.

Part 1
Ready, Set...

Ready, Set...

I do not want my house to be walled in on all sides and my windows to be stuffed. I want the cultures of all the lands to be blown about my house as freely as possible.

—Mahatma Ghandi

Traveling successfully with kids requires thoughtful itineraries, cultural preparedness, and light luggage. In this first section of the book, we outline the usual trip preparations with an eye toward details that are useful to families. Our philosophy is that the best trips happen when kids can take part in every phase of travel. Adults must make the final decisions: they have to book the plane tickets and make sure that the kids really have packed clean underwear. But kids can play an enormous role in all aspects of the planning and preparations.

In chapter one, we talk in detail about choosing a destination and an itinerary to suit your family's needs. How long should you stay in each spot? Should you take the red-eye and arrive early or fly all day and arrive at bedtime? What's the best way to book plane tickets online? We consider trade-offs such as budget, visas, and vaccinations in choosing a destination. It's not all dry details. We also cover fun topics such as locating creative lodging and finding interesting ways to move from town to town.

Even more important than preparing the travel logistics, is preparing your children. They will enjoy the trip more if they can visualize the places they will be visiting. The more they know, the happier they will be and the more they will get out of the trip. You can't expect them to be very excited about seeing a mosque when they don't know what it is. And, let's face it, art without previous exposure can be no fun at all. If you have read about the Mona Lisa, it's interesting to go and see her. If you stand in line to squint through glass at a painting of a lady that your parents tell you is really famous, it's going to be miserable (for all of you). In chapter two, we give you more ideas for preparing your kids than you will have time to try.

Chapter three addresses what to bring on your family's trip and, more importantly, what not to bring. The less you bring the easier it is to get around and the less you dread moving from place to place. Transportation between destinations is a major part of traveling which can be enjoyed, even cherished, rather than avoided due to heavy bags. While our book can help enrich a beach vacation where you might be able to pack the kitchen sink, what we offer is largely intended for the family that wants to move around. Leave the kitchen sink at home and just go.

1 Scoping the Journey

T ravel takes gumption. Amazing rewards can be found traveling with children, but family trips demand planning and effort. Different families will face different challenges. Some people can't imagine giving up the comforts of home. Others crave the sense of adventure and discovery that comes with traveling. Most people fall somewhere in the middle, wanting to see other places but unsure of how to step out the door.

Even though we had traveled extensively before having children, we were apprehensive about our first big family trip. "How much should we plan in advance? What will the kids eat? Will this even be fun?" Well, the trip was amazingly fun, in great part because we had prepared well in advance. As a result we were addicted to traveling with our kids. We found that well-planned travel was the perfect antidote to over-scheduled family life. In this chapter, we identify the big travel decisions and summarize the first steps in leaping out the door and onto that plane, train, or trail.

THE DESTINATION

You are ready to explore. You need to get out of town and see something new—and you're excited to take your kids. But where are you going to go? Sometimes the destination is already set: visiting relatives or extending a work-related trip to include a vacation. But if you have an open slate, there are number of factors to consider in making your decision.

One of the most exciting aspects of choosing a destination is the opportunity to explore culture and ecology. Exposing your kids to new people, languages, food, religion, art, politics, climates, animals, and ecosystems are likely some of the primary reasons you're interested in traveling in the first place. Just because you are traveling with kids doesn't mean that you need to limit yourselves to macaroni and cheese. There is adventure in different food, ancient history, and alternative life philosophies. Italy has pizza, Catholic churches, and cobblestone alleyways. Guatemala has black beans, animist Indians, and jungle pyramids. Japan has noodles, Buddhist temples, fast trains, and Hello Kitty. Search for cultures that appeal to both you and to your kids. Young learners are often more receptive to differences than adults, can pick up new languages faster than their parents, and—in most countries—can find familiar food basics. The key to successful travel is getting kids excited about what they will see, hear, smell, taste, and touch.

The second key aspect of choosing your destination is health and safety. You must be honest with yourself about your comfort level in visiting foreign cultures. Kids are susceptible to germs, dehydration, and food-borne bacteria. Different cultures have different ideas of what is safe. Balance your sense of travel adventure with your sense of travel risk. You will be able to find some form of health care anywhere you go, but standards vary widely, even in developed countries. Be particularly careful in choosing a destination for children with allergies, asthma, or other chronic medical conditions. Similarly, scheduling your trip to coincide with a political election could provide the excitement of seeing government in action, but your kids may not need to experience the unrest that might result. While it's important to keep safety in mind, do not let the worst-case scenario haunt you. We've seen ten-year-old kids hiking over high-mountain passes in remote areas of Nepal and families with infants in front packs wandering through Denali National Park. Letting your fears about what could happen dictate your itinerary will only result in a trip that is less than what your whole family is capable of experiencing and enjoying.

The third key aspect of choosing your destination is paperwork and political logistics. The majority of countries will allow most travelers through their ports for at least a brief amount of time, but the permitted length of stay can vary greatly depending on the destination and your country of origin. If you're planning a longer stay, or heading to somewhere rich in bureaucracy, you may require a visa ahead of your arrival. Check with the embassy of your potential destination or research visa requirements and travel limitations on the web. Consult the U.S. State Department for their travel recommendations (travel.state.gov).

Finally, the sad truth is that you probably have to consider your budget. Skiing in the Alps for four months might be nice but for most of us it's fairly unrealistic. However, a month in Southeast Asia might be within your means. Remember to subtract the costs of summer camps and childcare from the cost of your trip! Also note that some countries have helpful cost structures for children. Young children might be able to ride public transportation for free and are admitted to many museums free of charge. Check public transportation and museum websites as you choose between destinations.

THE ITINERARY

How long can you manage to be away from home? How many places do you want to visit? And how many days will you spend at each stop? Though keeping itineraries flexible is possible, a certain amount of planning will help set the kids' expectations and prevent travel disasters. Below are our top five recommendations for creating a successful family itinerary.

1. Involve your kids in the planning. Helping build your itinerary will give kids ownership of the trip. They will be more excited about a new place when they helped pick the destination, hotel, and method for getting there. Avoid questions like "Would you rather go to a gothic church or an amusement park?" because you already know the answer. Try organizing your trip around a theme such as "Castles," "The Life of Siddhartha," "The French Revolution," "The Route of Don Quixote," or "Rainforest Ecology." You set the framework and within that framework allow them to fine-tune the agenda and the details of the trip.

2. Don't travel every day. Moving from place to place uses up a lot of energy, and kids should not be expected to do it day after day. Even on a trip, kids may need to just hang out sometimes to feel grounded. Part of setting appropriate travel expectations is remembering that kids like to do their own thing. Down time can be a terrific addition to typical tourist itineraries. There are often neighborhood playgrounds with cool play structures that you don't see at home; even the pleasure of a simple swing can provide a perfect breather from the stress of traveling. Your kids are likely to interact with other kids at the park whether they can speak the same language or not. A restaurant

Don't underestimate the fun that comes with a new hotel room. It's a new home for a few days and it is just for your family. For you, it may be just another room with the same uncomfortable bed and off-white towels. But for the kids, it can be a whole new adventure: deciding who sleeps where, organizing their stuff onto shelves or drawers, and figuring out how to flush the toilet (not to mention the bidet). Little soaps, funny pillows, a breakfast buffet—new rooms every couple of days can be a source of fun in and of themselves, before you even get a chance to turn on the television.

can also be an oasis, allowing kids to renew their energy with food and drink. You can extend a restaurant rest period by breaking out the coloring books or playing a game at the table. The longer you stay, the more likely you will be to try a new flavor, chat with the folks at the table next to you, or enjoy some fun conversation with your server.

TRAVELING WITH OTHER FAMILIES

Traveling with other families offers a lot of fun for you and your kids, but it comes with trade-offs. You will probably be making these trade-off decisions from the beginning as you set your itinerary, plan your route, and buy your tickets, so you will need to be aware of them in advance.

Traveling with other families reduces the amount of quality time you get with your own children. The kids will likely spend more of their time together and less of their time with you. If you have younger kids, traveling with other families may make logistics unmanageable—different nap schedules, constant diaper changes, or an unruly pack of boys. It's also a lot harder to blend quietly into another culture as a larger group.

As your kids get older, bringing an extra child or traveling with another family may make the difference between a grumpy lone teenager and a happy group of willing young travelers. Pick other families and children that share the same travel style, and talk together (a lot!) about your expectations before you go.

When traveling with other families, we find it a big help to invest in tourist packages or to set an itinerary in advance. Tourist packages prevent on-the-spot, cross-family budget decisions, such as; "Is it okay to go to this museum even though the entrance fee is $15 per person?" The Salzburg Card, for example, is a big initial investment, but it provides entry into nearly every expensive attraction in Salzburg for 24 or 48 hours. No need to make the kids agree on the wax museum versus the Mozart House. You can do it all. And an itinerary is just another way to formalize expectations. It's no fun spending hours negotiating what to do next as a group.

On a long trip, it can be a wonderful relief to meet up with another family for a few days to share experiences, allow some play time for the kids, and enjoy grown-up conversation. Alphabet games with the kids at restaurants are great, but a beer, some jokes, and a little catching up with old friends is wonderful too. And remember, other traveling families that you meet on the road can also provide this sort of fun diversion.

3. Spend more time in each place. Traditional travel tours pack each day with activities from dawn to dusk to maximize the experience for the allotted time and money. But priorities are different when you are traveling with children. You don't want to miss the sights, but you also want every day to be fun. And let's be realistic: if it's not fun for the kids, it will not be fun for you. As you plan your itinerary, spending more time at a particular destination than most tour books recommend will allow you to avoid cramming traditional tourist activities into every minute.

4. Mix long and short destination stops. Planning your itinerary this way helps everyone recharge their energy after periods of more intense traveling. Spend only a day or two in Madrid seeing the Plaza Mayor and Museo del Prado but then spend five in Barcelona seeing the Ramblas and Sagrada Familia at a slower pace, spending more time in the park, and making time for an afternoon ice cream (or two) every day. Also remember that, as wonderful as the internet is, there is no substitute for on-the-ground information. When you arrive, you will undoubtedly discover more things you would like to see and do. Save time for these unexpected wonders.

5. Carry less stuff. The goal is to be quick and light. It's easier to move between destinations when you're not weighed down. Baby gear presents a particular challenge but it's surprising what you can live without. Toddlers can sleep on a quilt on the floor and, if you stick to buses and trains, you don't need a carseat. Since everything can be washed in a hotel sink, there is no need for lots of wardrobe changes for anyone in the family. We have traveled with everyone's belongings squished into a single backpack; the price of not having an extra blouse was well worth the reward of being able to wander from bus to funicular and from museum to market. We'll talk more about what to bring and who will carry it in chapter three.

THE PLANE TICKET

When it comes to airline travel, most choices are directly related to budget. Gone are the days when all airlines provided a reserved seat, a modest meal, and a movie. There are still airlines out there that offer these standards on every flight, but there are also luxury and budget airlines that offer much more or much less. Most airlines still have a class system in which first or business classes enjoy bigger seats, tastier food, and near bottomless alcohol. We can't give you much advice about first class, but we've walked past it many times on the way to our seats farther back and it sure looks nice.

Assuming you are not flying your whole family first class, should you fly on a standard airline or a budget airline? In order to compete in today's market, budget airlines have whittled away their services to the bare minimum. In some cases, these airlines load like school buses (the first one aboard gets to choose the seat) or charge for a glass of water. Budget airlines often apply fees to things you didn't know companies could charge for, such as speaking to a live person on the phone. If you are ready to jump these hurdles, budget airlines can be a good deal. But when traveling with children, the added charges on a budget airline (for seats together, for each bag of luggage, for food, for headphones) may make standard airlines economically competitive while also offering increased peace of mind.

BOOKING PLANE TICKETS

There are a zillion search engines out there, and the travel possibilities can be infinite and overwhelming. You could fly into Budapest and out of Rome or you could fly round trip to Vienna and take a train...

Here are just a few ideas to help you on your mission. Links to great search engines, online ticket auctions, and good travel deals are also found on our website: familyontheloose.com.

- Look for search engines that provide a range of dates so you can easily compare fares for different departure and arrival days.
- Register for fare alerts. Some airline search engines, such as kayak.com or orbitz.com, will alert you if fares dip below a particular threshold.
- For discount airlines in particular, you often get the best results by going directly to the airline website. Try Wikipedia's discount airlines page for a list of web links. Also search the phrase "discount airlines" and your destination.
- Some search engines (for example, kayak.com) provide information across multiple search engines and also track prices over time to help you determine if prices are falling or if they are at an all-time high.
- Note that some discount airlines do not guarantee flight times, so be careful if you have a tight schedule or if you are trying to link flights on two different airlines (and, of course, check back 24 hours in advance of departure to be safe).
- You can try auction-style sites like Priceline.com if you are willing to accept a number of connections or inconvenient flight times.
- The travel industry is always in flux. Pay attention to new incentives to get you into the plane and also new restrictions aimed at cutting airline costs.

Another common choice is how many travel legs you'll have on your way to your destination. Airlines often charge less for an itinerary that includes one or more stops along the way. Multiple stops do not have to be a negative, particularly if you have ample time. Sometimes stopovers allow you to explore a new place not originally on your itinerary. Stopovers of even a few minutes can be a big hassle, however, if you are traveling with an infant or a small child who still naps. Depending on the time of day and your child's age, you may have to wake your child at an awkward time to accomplish the plane-to-plane transfer. Transfers also increase the risk of missed connections if a flight is delayed. A direct flight may be worth a million dollars if it provides more rest and relaxation.

What time should you fly? Sometimes kids do well with really early flights. Put them to bed in their travel clothes and then just pop them into the car or taxi to the airport in the morning. Kids are often at their best in the morning, which helps the flight go smoothly. Overnight flights can also be nice because kids usually sleep, but remember that you also have to be able to sleep or they will arrive ready to go and you will be the one having the tired temper fit. The most important factor in deciding when to fly may be arrival time. If you are changing time zones, we strongly recommend arriving midday to help manage jetlag. When you arrive late, you will likely spend the better part of the night awake in the hotel. If you have to arrive at night, expect to spend the next day exhausted. Accepting jetlag and not worrying about being tired helps reduce stress, so plan your next-day itinerary accordingly.

Lastly, if you are interested in getting bumped (see "Getting Bumped" in chapter four) from an overbooked flight, the last flight of the day is best as airlines accumulate scheduling delays throughout the day and eventually have to either fit everyone into a plane or compensate them. Holidays and busy travel times can be unpleasant, but the likelihood of getting bumped increases.

THE LODGING

Choosing a place to sleep is both easier and harder than it used be. Though

> **INTERNET TRAVEL PLANNING TIP**
> Travel research and planning involves a lot of internet research. To make the most of it, you often have to provide vendors with your contact information. Set up a dummy e-mail address just for travel planning. You can minimize spam at your real e-mail address by using only the dummy address when you contact hotels, use lodging locators, order online, or join airline price watch services. The dummy account also helps organize all travel-related e-mails into a single place.

there are still times when it's fun to rely on the rogue guest house agents that solicit disembarking passengers, traveling with kids requires a little more foresight. The internet age brings many lodging options to your fingertips and can remove one of the stresses of arriving in a new place. However, there are usually many more choices on the ground than on the web. Decide first if you want to book every night's hotel or leave plans open and find lodging when you arrive. The first strategy may be most appropriate if you are traveling during the high season when the demand for rooms outstrips the supply. The latter strategy may

LOCATING LODGING

- Go to the bookstore or library and browse or buy several travel guides to get a feel for prices and possibilities. Note which types of lodging are recommended and any specific suggestions.
- Surf the internet for "lodging" and your destination name.
- Find out which options are conveniently located. Use free internet mapping sites such as MapQuest or Google Maps to locate the main landmarks you are interested in visiting and then scroll around for nearby lodging.
- Specifically search for B&Bs at your destination. B&B associations often list possible accommodations that don't have their own website.
- Try entering your lodging parameters into a lodging locator search engine for your destination to see what they come up with. We have had mixed luck with some fabulous finds, but also some annoying spam generation.
- Determine if the quality of the lodging is okay. Many traveler websites such as tripadvisor.com or room77.com include reviews of accommodations from other travelers. See what others in your situation think before you send your credit card for the deposit. Try searching for "traveler reviews" and your destination.
- Go to your destination's Chamber of Commerce website, Tourist Bureau site or their equivalent. Smaller establishments that do not have an independent web presence are often still listed through these types of agencies.
- Try searching for "hostel" or "short-term apartment rentals" for your destination. Other fun search words include "cabin," "cottage," "farm," "pilgrimage" (sometimes there can be rooms in monasteries for "pilgrims"), and "family."
- In big cities, you can often bid for lodging at big hotels. If you're feeling lucky, you can try Priceline.com or its equivalent and see what you can get for a little less.

work in the low season, in places where there is no travel season, or where the internet is not practical. A cursory internet check in advance is valuable in any case. You don't want to land on the Mediterranean coast in February only to find the whole town closed for the season.

A combination strategy is useful in hedging your bets. Try reserving a room for the first few nights of your trip and leaving your options open thereafter. This way you can get a sense of the local lodging market without committing too much in advance. If you don't book all your lodging in advance, you can use your own judgment about where you want to spend your time. Guidebooks are written for the generic traveler, not for your specific family. For example, Figueres, Spain, is described in one guidebook as a dump, only to be passed through on the way to somewhere else. But we arrived to find a small town with local flair, a kid-friendly Dali museum, a trail leading to a fort on the hill above town, and a cheap clown-themed hotel with a play area on the roof. Of course, we decided to spend the night!

Once you have decided on a booking strategy, being creative about lodging will help you maximize the fun for your fixed amount of time, energy, and money. Though a hotel outside the city may be cheaper, sleeping in a central location will ultimately put you closer to the things you came to see. Kids only have so much energy to expend in a day, and you will not want to spend all that energy just getting to the attraction. But be aware of the hazards of big cities too, such as traffic noise, loud revelers, and safety. You might not want to stay with your kids near Bangkok's Patpong Road or Amsterdam's red light district even though they are relatively centrally located.

Chances are you already know the comfort level of the lodging you desire based on your style and financial means. Whether you are planning to sleep in four-star luxury, hostel modesty, somewhere in between, or a mix of all options, the important thing is that you are comfortable. There are going to be days when your hotel room is your refuge, and you do not want to be fighting traffic noise, lumpy pillows, or bedbugs to get your rest. A lot of folks can sleep through anything, but that may not be much of an asset if they cannot get to sleep in the first place. Some big city hotels advertise soundproof windows, a nifty feature when you are jetlagged or in need of a midday rest.

There is something to be said for buying in bulk, and beds are no exception. A hostel is often the cheapest option for the single traveler, but that may not be the case for a family. Many hotels offer family rooms or apartments that are slightly larger than their normal rooms and may be similar in cost, or even cheaper, than hostel beds for four. If traveling with teenagers, two rooms may be more expensive than a family room but worth their weight in gold in terms of privacy and independence. We also need to point out that, while comfort is obviously important, you don't want boring lodging. You can stay at the Holiday Inn when you visit Great Aunt Mabel in Springfield, but here is your chance to try something different. The tiny room in the historic inn with the bathroom down the hall, the drafty apartment in a 300-year-old monastery, or the Japanese tatami room are memories your kids will not soon forget. A little discomfort can also help your kids build confidence in their own ability to manage life's ups and downs.

Explore the creative options. For stays of more than two or three days, you can rent a furnished apartment, an extra room in a private home, or even arrange a home exchange. Apartments come with kitchens for quick and cheap access to kid food 24 hours a day. Homestays and home exchanges may bring you closer to the local culture. And there are other options, too. Universities often rent empty dormitory rooms when school is not in session. Some regions specialize in farm stays. Monasteries and church organizations often have rooms for rent (very quiet) and pubs sometimes have rooms upstairs (perhaps a bit loud). Learn how different forms of lodging are referred to in the places you are going (for example: pension, hostel, gasthof) so that you do not overlook some of the options.

TRANSPORTATION ON THE ROAD

You will probably be flying on a plane to reach your first destination, but you will have choices of transportation between stops on your trip. Keep in mind that the fastest, easiest, or cheapest way may not be the best or the most exciting for your kids. Be creative in getting from one place to another. Some transport can be booked in advance while other methods require a flexible spirit. It is way more fun to take an overnight train or ferry between cities than to climb into another rental car and jump on another highway. The extent and quality of public transportation varies all over the world, from smelly, crowded buses to trains with dining cars and velvet seats. Calculate that you would be saving the cost of one night's lodging, and it may not be all that expensive to take an overnight train with your own private couchette. On one leg of a trip in Japan, we took a bus, funicular, gondola, pirate boat, and train from one hotel to another—not the fastest way, but it sure was fun!

Unless you specifically plan a rural component into your trip, traveling between cities may be the only exposure your kids have to local agriculture, forests, and mountains. Natural areas are important components of a region's cultural, environmental, and economic identity. Seeing rice paddies, vineyards, and wheat fields out of the window, or conversely, smoke stacks, shanty slums, and

CAMPING AND CAMPER VANS

- Camping is an economical option in many countries. And the experience brings surprising cultural differences. Did you know, for example, that you can have fresh bread delivered to your German campsite on Sunday mornings? Many European campsites are less-than-private (to put it nicely) but they often have hot showers, stainless steel indoor kitchens, and espresso stands!
- Campgrounds can be investigated in advance with Google Earth.
- If you don't want to lug all your camping equipment, consider renting a camper van. The kids will love sleeping in the bunks and you can save money by cooking and sleeping on the road. It also gives you a good excuse to explore local grocery stores—often a trip highlight. You won't be quite as comfortable exploring the narrow back roads of old villages in a big camper, but the trade-off may be worth it for a few days of cheap outdoor enjoyment.
- Many major rental car companies also rent camper vans. Private rentals may be cheaper and we have had some great luck. However, you should use caution in arranging any private internet deals, especially if it means you need to show up in a foreign country with a pocket full of cash to make a deposit with someone you've never met.

suburban sprawl, can provide insights into the region's history and development, sparking family conversations about the differences between here and home.

Renting a car frees you from the train or bus schedule and offers you the freedom to go places that might otherwise be inaccessible. Cars also carry your stuff and limit the distances you have to walk. If you are traveling with many children, renting a car may be your most economical choice. Even for a small family, renting a car saves on bus and train tickets and enables you to stay at less expensive lodging out of the city center. But as always, there are trade-offs (see "Renting a Car"). One parent must drive the car and another is often involved in navigation. That doesn't leave much extra parent attention for the flock of children in the back seat. We recommend that you not rent a car for the whole international adventure since trains, trams, ferries, and buses can be so exciting.

HEALTH PREPARATIONS

No matter where you are, your health and your children's health are one of your primary responsibilities. Just as at home, you should be prepared to take care

RENTING A CAR

There are a number of logistical issues to consider when renting a car. Many countries require drivers to have an international driver's license. An international driver's license is simply a translation of your current driver's license and it can typically be obtained for a small fee from driving associations either at home or on the road. Make sure to check official sources such as local governments or your own embassy website for licensing requirements. Rental car companies are eager for your business and may make the legal requirements sound more lenient than they really are. Investigate whether you need to buy a pass in advance for highway travel or for toll roads and bridges.

Check the driving laws in every country where you plan to drive. In Slovenia, for example, you are required to drive with your lights on at all times. It is also compulsory to carry a reflective vest, a warning triangle, and first aid kit. There are steep fines for missing equipment. One wonders how much money the country takes in per year from visitors who aren't aware of these laws. Also make sure that you are insured. Your insurance company at home may cover you when driving abroad, but it is more likely that you will have to purchase additional coverage. We've heard horror stories about hidden and expensive red tape after an accident. Read the fine print in the rental contract.

Most rental car companies will include, for a small fee, children's safety seats. It can be a hassle bringing safety seats from home, but if you want them for the plane anyway, you can save a little money by supplying them yourself. You don't want to be stuck, however, having to carry them around for the legs of your trip when you are not renting a car.

Automobile preferences and standards differ across the world, and there are few places where cars are bigger than in North America. Our visiting friend from Austria showed us a funny picture she had taken on her first day in the U.S. What was so funny? A parking sign that said "Small Cars Only" with a Toyota RAV4 parked in front. Apparently she hadn't seen a Ford Excursion yet. Infrastructures, like the width of roads and parking spaces, reflect the average car size. So, renting a big SUV like the one you have at home may not be very practical in, for example, Japan. Also note that, in some places, cars with automatic transmissions can be twice as expensive to rent than cars with standard transmissions.

of scrapes and minor illnesses yourself, but you need a back-up plan for more serious situations. Always review your health plans with your own physician and your child's pediatrician before you go and, if possible, get a referral for a doctor or clinic at your destination. We'll talk about on-the-road safety considerations in chapter five but the vast majority of health-related work will ideally happen during the planning stages.

To prevent illness and injury, you need to research the risks of your destinations in detail. Informing yourself about conditions and health risks around the world is relatively easy. Your physician or local travel clinic can provide up-to-date information on health risks and necessary immunizations. The Centers for Disease Control and Prevention also maintains a great website for travelers (wwwnc.cdc.gov/travel) with worldwide health information. Note that unfamiliar vaccines may be recommended even in developed countries. If you need vaccinations, visit a travel clinic well in advance of your trip (at least three months ahead,

TRAVEL TIP: EMERGENCY BRACELETS AND ALLERGY ALERTS

Two months ahead of your trip, order engraved medical ID bracelets with emergency contact information in case your kids get lost. You usually get three-to-four lines of text and you can fill these with a hotel phone number, a local friend's phone number, or your international cell phone number. Save one line for a contact phone number at home. Not your home number of course, since you won't be there, but the phone number of someone who can help manage an emergency remotely. Note that, more than once, our child's ID bracelets have also been our quickest solution to lost contact information such as misplacing a friend's phone number or not being able to locate a hotel.

These ID bracelets can be ordered online. Your local pharmacy might also have order forms for inexpensive medical ID bracelets. If there is medical information that your child should have on them at all times, include that information too, preferably in the language of your destination. There's nothing wrong with wearing two bracelets.

If you or your child has a serious allergy, it will be very helpful to have a bracelet or a letter translated with the explanation "I am allergic to ____. If I eat ____, I may die." Show it to every waitperson to reduce the chances of exposure.

if possible) as some vaccines require a series of shots to be effective. You may also want to ask your doctor or the travel clinic for prescription medicines to take with you. For example, we always travel with a broad-spectrum antibiotic in less-developed regions. The kids have to be weighed to adjust the dose each time. Luckily, we have had to throw the unused medications out after each trip but, if we ever were to have a quickly spreading skin infection or an intolerable bladder infection, we would have had a little extra time to get trained help.

If there are particular health considerations for you or your children (for example, asthma, allergies to food or insects, susceptibility to particular bacteria such as strep, frequent migraines, irritable bowel syndrome) that require special medications, stock up before you go. And remember to consider special safety equipment that you might need for your kids. Bring a well-fitting life jacket for each child if you plan to island hop in Thailand, a good helmet for horseback riding or a bike trip, and a carseat or booster seat for car rides, especially in less-developed countries. Though many places will rent this equipment, we strongly recommend that you bring your own if you are unsure or have questions about their quality and cost.

Finally, to prevent budgetary disasters, you need to ensure that you and your children are covered by health insurance for the duration of the trip. Many, but not all, major carriers include some world coverage. Call first or check your insurance company's website to be sure. It is pretty easy to buy short-term traveler's insurance for major medical coverage, too. Check the internet or ask your insurance agent for a trusted company. Note that these policies rarely cover nonemergency care.

Of course, you will also need to bring a travel first-aid kit. This travel first-aid kit is a physical embodiment of an oxymoron—you want to pack small and light while being prepared for every possible accident or health need. You want a full-service drugstore compressed into a tiny cube. We discuss in great detail what to pack in this kit in chapter three.

We hope we never need it but it is always good to have a contingency plan, like a referral for a physician or hospital you can communicate with and trust. In many developed, English-speaking destinations, you will be able to find emergency or urgent care with a phone book or some help from the hotel clerk. If you do not speak the language or you are not totally comfortable with the local health care system, you may want to get a physician or hospital referral in advance. You can get a referral from a friend or a friend's family in your destination country, from your own physician, or from your country's embassy or consulate. You can also check the internet in advance from home, as you may not have either the access or the composure to search carefully in the event of a real emergency. On arrival in any country, remember to check the emergency phone number, as it is not always 911.

PASSPORTS, VISAS, AND OTHER PAPERWORK

Deal with bureaucratic issues well in advance of your proposed departure because they may take a long time to resolve and because having them complete will relieve some pretravel stress. Dealing with kids' papers only compounds the time requirements and headaches. Leave plenty of time to get through the bureaucracy. Getting or updating a passport these days can take months, depending on how much time, energy, and money you can invest in the process. Kids' passports often expire sooner than adults, so make sure everyone's passport will be current for the duration of the trip. Note that expedited passport services are available in some areas but these expedited services are often very expensive and may be reserved only for citizens with a plane ticket that is already purchased.

To speed up visa paperwork, check your destination country's website for required paperwork and make sure you send everything they request. You can also e-mail the consulate or embassy to ask questions before you send in the forms. Extra forms and headaches may be required for adopted children or non-traditional family structures. Be patient but do not give up. With your persistence, bureaucracies will adapt. If you are really in a hurry for a visa, e-mail your circumstances in advance and then send a prepaid return express mail (UPS, USPS, or FedEx) envelope with your materials.

Other paperwork you should consider carrying with you on your trip includes the kids' birth certificates (to confirm that they are indeed your children), vaccination records (to remind you that they are covered against hepatitis B or whatever), and any health-related information that a doctor may need in case of an emergency. For young children, it's a great idea to get ID bracelets with emergency telephone numbers etched on the inside (see "Travel Tip: Emergency Bracelets and Allergy Alerts").

BUDGETS

Many budget decisions have to be made during the trip preparations: Where are you going? How long can you afford to be away? What major activities can you count on? What kind of lodging will you be using? Most choices will ultimately involve affordability and during the pre-trip planning period is a good time to introduce the idea of a budget to your children. Get those financial realities out there such as allowances, splurge possibilities or impossibilities, and budget limits.

If your kids help with planning, they will figure out that if you choose the expensive hotel, you may not be able to go to the amusement park or fancy restaurant. Although life is full of these kinds of trade-off decisions, when traveling your consequences are generally immediate and you usually have the chance to try a better budgeting scheme the next day or in the next town. Involving your children in these financial decisions is a great way to teach them your values and to provide them with more experience in real life decision-making.

Whenever possible, give your kids the real cost of several alternatives and let them choose (or at least vote). For example, explain that you can stay in Mexico for only six nights in the three-star hotel on the beach that costs $130 per night, or you can stay for eight nights in a hotel without so many amenities and a short walk from the beach ($95 per night). Or would they prefer to stay at the cheaper hotel for only six nights and go see the Mayan ruins for four nights instead of only two?

TRAVEL INSURANCE

Buy it or skip it? Travel insurance, or trip cancellation insurance, generally reimburses you for otherwise nonrefundable costs in the event of particular emergencies. Each policy differs somewhat in what is covered and in what constitutes an emergency. Many policies include extra bells and whistles such as lost luggage insurance and damaged property insurance.

Travel insurance can be purchased with your plane ticket or it can be purchased as a stand-alone insurance policy via multiple companies. To find a reputable company, check with your insurance agent or search the internet carefully. The advantage of travel insurance is that you can get most of the costs of your trip returned if you are unable to travel for certain reasons. Again, policies differ in what reasons they allow but they usually include things like major illness or accidents, weather emergencies, wars, or airline strikes. The more people you travel with, the more likely it is that someone will get sick or injured; however, the more people you travel with, the more expensive the policy. Definitely check your policy to be sure that everyone's costs are covered if one person can't travel. For example, if one parent breaks a leg ten hours before departure, is it only his or her costs that are covered and the rest of the family is expected to go on alone? Read the fine print and compare several possible reputable vendors.

If you are considering travel insurance, you may also want to check with your credit card companies; some offer insurance that functions much like travel insurance on anything purchased with that card (including the airline tickets, hotel deposits, etc.). Also, many travel health insurance policies carry some limited trip cancellation insurance.

We travel frequently and have never opted to buy extra travel insurance. Our logic is that eventually we will end up losing money because we have to cancel a trip, but the cost savings of never having bought insurance will be greater in the long run. However, circumstances differ with every trip and with every family. If you must make a very large deposit, consider travel insurance. Or if travel insurance will buy you peace of mind, maybe it's worth every penny even if you don't end up needing it.

Just Go!

It may seem like there are a lot of decisions and logistics for your first big trip, but it's all very manageable if you start early (see "The Big Trip Planning Timeline"). Once you get the hang of it and you have some experience, you can whittle the prep work down to the bare minimum (see "The Spontaneous Trip Planning Timeline"). Share and enjoy the planning with your kids. Share and enjoy the research, packing, and saving with them as well. It's all part of the adventure and the education. Of all that you do for your kids, memories and insights learned traveling may be some of the things that they remember the most vividly and cherish the most fondly.

THE BIG TRIP PLANNING TIMELINE

Four to six months predeparture	Research destinations (culture, health and safety, political logistics, costs, etc.).
Four months predeparture	Book plane tickets; order passports; visit travel clinic/pediatrician; splurge on a travel guide.
Three months predeparture	Settle on an itinerary and book lodging; arrange within-trip transportation; check that you have health insurance; decide if you want travel insurance.
Two months predeparture	Apply for visas; start preparing the kids (see chapter two); check out juvenile nonfiction, fiction, and activity books related to your destination and its language; order ID bracelets with emergency contact information.
One month predeparture	Check packing list (see chapter three) and purchase any necessary travel stuff (gear, clothes, walking shoes, first aid, etc.); arrange a housesitter to manage mail, care for pets, and pay bills while you are away.
Two weeks predeparture	Start gathering items you plan to pack into a pile; check airline for carry-on and checked baggage limitations; start accumulating essential paperwork.
One week predeparture	Remove half the items you plan to pack from the pile and then try to fit remaining items in your backpack/suitcase (there should be extra room!); photocopy important papers (including pages from this book); print all your essential trip e-mails (plane itinerary, lodging reservations, etc.); visit a destination restaurant and practice a few words; wrap up little plane presents (see chapter four).
The night before	Write a letter for the housesitter; send your travel contact information to someone (if you really do want to be reached in an emergency!); pack your bags; prepare the carry on bags (see chapter four).

THE SPONTANEOUS TRIP PLANNING TIMELINE

Two to four weeks predeparture	Search up information about a destination (research cultural opportunities, safety and health, logistics); book plane tickets and the first few days of lodging at each stop; initiate kid preparation and check a language tape out of the library; call the housesitter; apply for visas and visit the travel clinic if necessary.
Two weeks predeparture	Check travel supplies and stock up if necessary; start piling up the things you want to bring with you (see chapter three); check closet for plane gifts (see chapter four).
The night before	Pack luggage and plane bag (including gifts and snacks); grab essential paperwork.

2 Sowing Seeds of Enthusiasm

Preparation builds kids' travel enthusiasm. The statue of David in Florence, for example, is going to be anticlimactic if you have never heard of it, and a Shinto shrine is not very different from a pretty park unless you know something about Japanese religion. Cultural preparation through pre-trip crafts, library visits, cultural events, and dining can essentially extend your trip from weeks of travel into months of fun. Maps, restaurants, DVDs, cultural performances or celebrations, slide shows, lectures, fiction or nonfiction books, and friends who have already been to your destination can all be portals to adventure. Don't worry about spoiling the surprises. Kids love familiar patterns. How many times can they watch a movie before they begin to get tired of it? And no matter how much you prepare, there will always be surprises, big and small, which is, for us, one of the best reasons to travel in the first place. Devoting pretravel time to cultural exploration will pay off in spades the first time your kid says something like, "The first thing I want to do in Paris is to see the Little Dancer!"

In this chapter, we explore activities that open your children's eyes to the cultures and environments they will experience on their upcoming trip. Advanced exposure will help set their expectations and provide a foundation for exploration on the road. First we will talk about initial investigations into the culture and places you will visit: including reading the stories, learning the language, and eating the food. Then we'll describe a few neat big-picture activities to organize your trip: making a calendar or itinerary, creating a map of your proposed route, and creating a budget.

READ, WATCH, AND LISTEN

Your library is a one-stop shop for travel preparedness. It's easy to tap into the vast array of books, DVDs, and music that is compiled in most libraries. Plenty of media is geared toward children, but specialized resources about your destination may be aimed at adults. Be prepared to do some advanced filtering or act as an information conduit for your kids; being a conduit has the extra advantage of helping you prepare and get excited, too.

There are travel books out there for almost every country or region. They are written for everyone from backpackers seeking hostels to first-class passengers looking for four-star hotels. You already know the type of travel you're planning for this next trip so choose books that fit your needs. Although many of the library books will have outdated hotel prices and restaurant ratings, general background information changes slowly or not at all. You can find great summaries of local history and ecology in most travel guides and many are packed with glossy pictures that your children will want to flip through and explore. Once you've determined which travel guide you want to bring along, you can purchase the most up-to-date edition at your local travel bookstore, independent bookseller, or online.

Apart from travel guides, many other nonfiction books will also be useful to you. Juvenile nonfiction is often more fun and colorful even for adults (or maybe it's just us). Your local library or your children's school library is the best place to start. There are juvenile nonfiction books about almost every country in the world and all the major cities. Look for books on the history of a region, art from a local artist or movement, religion, or biographies of famous people. Also check for books about time periods, historical events, or ancient cultures that will be relevant on your trip, such as Mayan civilizations, the Middle Ages, the French Revolution, or World War II. Books about particular landmarks, such as the Eiffel Tower in Paris, or historical figures, such as Hans Christian Anderson when from Denmark, can also be engaging. Our daughters guided us through the Van Gogh museum in Amsterdam after reading books about him at their school library. Although you will want to search out unique, subtle, or strange cultural tidbits once you arrive, your family will benefit from prior exposure to and excitement about the big icons.

Don't forget that works of fiction are set everywhere in the world, too. Many of these books, particularly folk and fairy tales, are specifically for children and can inspire all sorts of intercultural curiosity. There are classics like The Jungle Book (India), Madeline (Paris), Tom Sawyer (The Mississippi Valley), Anne of Green Gables (Nova Scotia), and The Little Mermaid (Copenhagen). And don't forget Asterix or Tintin and his international detective adventures if you are headed to France! There are also thousands of lesser-known stories set in exciting locations.

The librarian for the children's section should be able to help you refine your search. Some of our favorites include a crepe seller who tours Paris, a shy boy growing up in northeastern Thailand, and circus twins solving mysteries in Amsterdam. The best books describe specific physical landmarks, local foods, or celebrations that you might be lucky enough to witness.

DVDs of both travelogues and fictional stories are also a fun way to preview the trip. They are especially intriguing when produced in the country you will visit. Americanized stories about other cultures don't always portray life accurately. You'll likely find more at a large public library than at a chain video store or an internet retailer. There are short videos at the public library on places, history, cities, people, and ecology in addition to longer in-depth films. Often, a twelve-minute mini-documentary is just what you need.

> **PREPARATION TIP: WALK BEFORE YOU GO!**
>
> Most travel involves walking— usually more walking than you do at home. By practicing walking longer distances at home, you'll get the whining over with on your own turf. Whether your child is in a stroller or is a teenager with longer legs than you, set walking expectations in advance. Walk to the grocery store, tour your own city as a tourist might, or set up a long scavenger hunt around the neighborhood. It'll help get leg muscles and mind muscles in good walking shape, and it'll help you all be prepared for one of travel's big challenges ("Walking" in chapter five).

Although American music is heard almost everywhere in the world, there are many musical styles and dances unique to particular countries that the kids will hear and see on your trip. Teens and tweens may especially enjoy exploring regional pop music. Check out the international music collection at your library. You cannot go to Vienna without hearing Strauss and trying to waltz, to Spain without flamenco, or anywhere in India without the movies and music of Bollywood.

SPEAK UP!

Unless you are going someplace extremely remote, it should be possible to give your children prior experience with the languages they will hear on your trip. Again, the library is a free, and convenient bet. You can also find foreign language exposure at your child's school, at bookstores, at an ethnic restaurant, or even a karate dojo. At the very least, you and the kids should learn a few basic phrases that you will either hear spoken or have to speak to be polite or to get something that you want. It's an important lesson for your kids that, even though English is everywhere in the tourist world, the tourist also bears language responsibility. The absolute basics include:

- Hello/Goodbye
- Please/Thank you/You're welcome
- I would like …
- Excuse me/I'm sorry
- Numbers up to one hundred
  A few phrases that come in surprisingly handy:
- Delicious!
- Where is the bathroom?
- Can you help me please?
- Is this okay? (Useful for any number of situations)
- Where is the…?
- Left, right, straight, stop
- What's your name? My name is…
- Where are you from? I am from…
- How old are you? I am…years old.

You can learn a language on many free internet sites (see our website for ideas) or you can buy or borrow language recordings. Language recordings that include songs are particularly helpful in getting children excited to learn another language. Most public libraries carry a wide variety of options. Some even rent language-learning software or will provide access to language-learning software via the internet with a library card number.

Apart from reading and listening to recordings, you can also take a language course. Unfortunately, not many of these courses will be specifically geared for kids even though kids can learn languages much faster than adults. Another option is to hire a tutor who can design a customized program for your family. For convenience, the tutor may even come to your home and provide some cultural lessons too (on purpose or by accident). A native-speaking tutor will provide exposure to English as spoken by people at your destination. Tutors need not be expensive or even professional; they just need to be able to help you and your family gain exposure to the sounds of the words and learn a few basic phrases. Tutors can be your neighbors, foreign students at the local community college, the daughter of a visiting professor, or the friendly young waiter at the local ethnic restaurant.

Local schools, community colleges, and universities often offer home-stay programs for international students or interns. These can run for a few days (when the student first arrives), or a couple of weeks while the student is introduced to our culture and she finds her own place to live, or for the entire semester. If you find a local program and a student from your destination, you can trade a place to stay and an introduction to your own culture for a glimpse into the language and customs of their culture. We offer more ideas about cultural exchanges in chapter nine.

EAT, COMER, ESSEN, TABETAI!

Food is a delicious window into culture. Explore ethnic restaurants in your neighborhood to taste foods that you might find on your trip. If the menu is unfamiliar to you, ask the server what the typical staple diet includes and what the "comfort" foods are. It is great to be adventurous when trying new food, but the local "mac and cheese" may become your kids' favorite food on the road. In most places, comfort food includes some form of noodles, rice, or soup, which your kids will probably recognize and welcome. Prior familiarity with the region's flavors will make eating there more fun and less intimidating. Different areas will probably have new fruits and vegetables to try. Though they're probably not so healthy, there are also likely fantastic new pastries, desserts, and candy, too.

If you're feeling brave, you can even cook local food at home. Search

CULTURAL PREPAREDNESS

There are cultural subtleties everywhere. Discovering these differences in advance can be tricky. Often the only way to uncover them is to ask a native or a well-traveled friend. A great question is "What are the negative stereotypes about foreigners?" For example, in Japan foreigners are known to take up way too much space on trains and to be very loud. Once you know this, you can actively tuck your bags under your seat, keep your elbows in, lower your voice, and encourage your kids to do the same. In many parts of Asia, the bottom of your foot is the rudest part of the body. One would no more sit with the bottom of the foot pointing at someone in Thailand than one would sit with his or her rear end toward someone in the U.S. In some cultures personal space is very big, while in others it is nonexistent. Modesty also varies widely between countries. Talk to your kids in advance about these differences, and prepare them to observe them on the road. Help them understand that they are ambassadors for their own culture. Their journal will be a neat place to track these differences and traditions en route (see chapter seven).

the internet for ideas and recipes, and then your local grocery stores or ethnic convenience stores for the ingredients. Many large grocery stores have an ethnic food section if you want to avoid making everything from scratch. Include the kids in the kitchen because they love to measure things and taste the fruits of their labor. Even if you don't get it quite right, you at least have a basis for an eating expedition on your trip. The whole family will be motivated to taste tamales, for example, to compare to the ones you made at home. Also, identify foods that you can't find or make at home to generate excitement about trying them on the road, such as orchid ice cream in Turkey or durian fruit in Malaysia.

CELEBRATE SOMETHING NEW

A wonderful way to get an authentic taste of a region's culture is through holidays and local community festivals. Often holidays and festivals include traditional clothes or foods and they are rarely just for tourists. Some holidays will already be familiar to you, but often they'll have a new flavor unique to a particular region. Other holidays will be completely new, especially if you are visiting a region whose dominant religion is different from your own. Wonderfully, many holidays will seem downright wacky. What an adventure it could be for you and your kids to see something truly silly, surprising, or unbelievable.

If you live in a medium-sized or large city, pay attention to the cultural events section of your local newspaper. Often immigrant communities continue to celebrate their holidays and festivals in their new country. This might allow you to enjoy traditional music, dance, food, and costumes before you go—and you could try speaking a few words of that new language you have been learning. People from all over the world are excited to share their heritage, so tell them that you are on your way to visit their homeland and perhaps you will gain invaluable travel tips.

You can look for regional celebrations in books and on the internet, but the information may not do the festival justice. An advantage of a flexible itinerary is the possibility of changing destinations or staying longer to enjoy these unexpected events. Unique holidays and celebrations we have found include Songkran (mid-April), Chinese Vegetarian Festival (October), and Loy Krathong (November) in Thailand, Saint John the Baptist Day (late June) in Spain, Independence Day (September 15–16) in Guatemala and Mexico, and Diwali (October or November) in Nepal and India. There are countless others just as interesting.

GET CRAFTY!

Arts and crafts are big slices of the cultural pie. Every area of the world is known for a form of art or a special craft. Many crafts even become regional symbols, such as Swiss cuckoo clocks, wooden shoes from the Netherlands, or Thai silk. Traditional craft items might be available as mementos or souvenirs of a trip. You will probably see them for sale in gift shops all along the way and you may even be able to observe them being made at a folk art museum, an outdoor museum, or a festival. What arts or crafts are made along your route? Surf the internet with word combinations such as your destination and "folk," "folk art," "traditional," "artisan," "craft," or "art." Again, you can get a lot of cool ideas at your library. You may be lucky enough to find a craft book specific to your destination or find unique ideas by browsing through books that cover crafts from around the world.

Once you know what crafts you are likely to see *en route,* try making them with your kids. Craft books at the library probably have instructions for hands-on activities. If not, search the internet again for "curriculum" or "how-to" and the craft you want to make. If you will be traveling around any major holidays, you

CRAFT IDEAS FOR COMMON DESTINATIONS

Australia: Paint a rock using only tiny dots in the aboriginal style.

Canada: Sew or glue a canoe out of the bark from trees in your own back yard or make an Inukshuk from rocks.

England: Make crowns from tinfoil and plastic gems or design and draw a family shield representing your own family's history, characteristics, and values.

Guatemala: Make little worry dolls from pipe cleaners and scraps of cloth.

India: Try your hand at paper mache masks or thread strings of glass beads.

Indonesia: Create shadow puppets out of tag board and colored cellophane.

Japan: Make wind socks in the form of fish or a clay Maneki Neko ("beckoning cats").

Mexico: Create black clay pots or Day of the Dead masks.

Pacific Northwest, U.S.: Create a totem pole using construction paper, markers, and a poster tube.

Russia: Paint an old wooden picture frame with gold and black paint.

Thailand: Weave a simple basket or try making a tekraw ball.

Venice and Brazil: Decorate a carnival-style mask with glitter and feathers.

can also find out about special holiday crafts or decorations to be on the lookout for, such as hand-painted Easter eggs in Salzburg, paper Christmas stars in Denmark, or a flower boat for Loy Krathon if you're visiting Thailand in November. Other good resources include the art teacher at your children's school, a home schooling center in your area, or a craft supply store. Bring along a color photo of what you want to make and see what ideas the art experts have or what materials might work to create something similar. Once you have the supplies, make the project special. Put on regional music, set out some regional snacks, and enjoy your crafting adventure. Your kids will be so much more excited to see the real thing.

SET THE AGENDA

A calendar can be so many things. First, it'll help you organize the travel preparations (for example, set a date to get passport photos taken all together, schedule language lessons, or finish shopping see "The Big Trip Planning Timeline" in chapter one). Include kids' pretravel tasks on the calendar and check off chores as they are finished. Second, a calendar can help you keep track of itinerary details. For example, you can write your planned location on each date and underline those dates for which you have room reservations. When you book transportation on the road, make additional lodging reservations, plan to meet another family, or schedule an excursion, it'll really help if you can glance up and see the whole trip displayed on the wall. Third, it'll help your kids get ready for their upcoming journey. Have them number the days and label each one with the city where you plan to be. Younger kids can use stickers. Also label the day you arrive back home. Have younger kids draw a picture of their own house on this date. Once on the road, this familiar drawing on a fixed date will help them manage anxiety and homesickness.

You can make or buy a special trip calendar. Ideally, it should be big enough to mount on the fridge or post on the wall for easy reference before you go. But it should also be small enough to fold up and bring to follow along as you go and to prepare for what is coming up next. A big sheet of paper with hand-drawn lines should do the trick—the bigger the squares for each day, the better. You can also print a calendar out on the computer or tape the necessary months together from a store-bought calendar. In any case, keep it where your kids can see it.

MAP IT OUT!

Creating a map of your destination begins to give your kids a sense of what traveling really means. The best place to start is with a globe. Since two-dimensional maps are intrinsically distorted, globes are the best spatial representation of the earth. The three-dimensional shape will help them understand that they are not just going from one spot on a map to another, but are actually traveling to a different part of the round Earth. A globe can also help demonstrate and explain time zone changes and why some flights between North America and Europe take you close to the North Pole while others veer further south. In examining a globe, your children will likely come up with other surprising questions.

Technological advances in recent years have improved our ability to see our destination ahead of time. You can now use Google Earth to "fly" over your home and destination. You can even use this tool to explore your actual trip route. You can go up to 10,000 feet and track along the flight path, zooming in to examine interesting or confusing landmarks along the way. Visit NASA's Landsat website (landsat.gsfc.nasa.gov) and search for images of your destination.

Once you have gained the global perspective, you'll want to focus in on your destination region and country. Find a map or two that shows your entire travel area in detail, but don't get too focused on just that one region. Even if you are only going to the southern part of Thailand, for example, it's good to get a map of the whole country so that you can see your destination or route in the context of the entire political and cultural landscape. Good travel bookstores have maps of every spot on Earth, and you can buy maps of any location online. Though the internet itself is also a handy tool, nothing beats spreading out a good old-fashioned paper map on the kitchen table.

With paper map in hand, you can outline your proposed route. Talk about geography, such as neighboring countries, mountain ranges, seas, or deserts. The map will lend itself to a wide range of topics. Go into as much depth as you and your children want. Use the map as a jumping off point to identify religious boundaries, where different languages are spoken, how and why political borders have changed over time, and how tectonic plates work to form mountain ranges. These conversations may dovetail perfectly with the books you have already checked out from the library. These discussions could even send you back to the library for more. Your children will ask you questions you can't possibly answer off the top of your head.

You can also use the map for logistics planning. Go over the alternatives for how you can get from one place to another, and discuss which one is best for your family. If you set your itinerary in advance, trace it out with a yellow highlighter. Add blue highlighter when you travel to mark your progress. If you plan to wing it, just bring the map and the highlighter with you—they'll pack easily. Are you or the kids feeling super-compulsive? Hang the map next to the calendar and color code your route and your calendar. The map makes a great memento for when you get home and want to show your friends exactly where you went (see chapter eight). If you really want to make the most of your map, check out our mapping and measurement curriculum on our website to add a little math to the mix.

Count Your Money

You have worked together on the overall trip budget. But what about the kids' own spending money? They are never too young to appreciate the trade-offs and subtleties of a limited wallet. Even if you don't think shopping will be a major part of your agenda, we can almost guarantee that there will be financial temptations for your youngsters. If you are going somewhere so remote that no enterprising local has figured out how to separate tourists from their cash, congratulations! Otherwise, expect to be subjected to traditional crafts, postcards, candy, souvenirs, books, rides, and junk (often the same junk you find at home but with enticingly different packaging).

Your kids should share in the idea that there is not a bottomless supply of money for your trip. A budget spreadsheet can help us all see how far our money can (or can't) go. Fill out our "Sample Budget Spreadsheet" before you go and then use it on the road by pasting it into the back of a travel journal. Track how close you were to your estimates. You could also use our sample spreadsheet to inspire a conversation or for the creation of a more detailed, customized spreadsheet. To make it more interesting for the kids, include their allowance or help them to create their own spreadsheet. Spreadsheets and budget planning may not prevent your children from wanting to buy every

Preparation Tip: Put Your Kids in Charge!

The above ideas help you prepare your kids for learning on the road. What about teaching your kids to prepare themselves? Try creating a preparation scavenger hunt. Take them to the library and have them find the answers to a series of questions about your destination. If they are older still, put all the learning in their hands. Tell them that they are invited on an expedition and, in order to participate, they must complete a set of tasks. Examples of tasks could be to make a timeline of what has happened on the Sinai Peninsula over the past 1,000 years, identify three locations in South Africa that have historical significance, or create a species list of plants and animals in Costa Rica. Have each child complete a different task and share their results with the whole family.

trinket in the first tchotchke shop you see, but it will at least help you frame an argument on why they can't.

Discuss what your children might see, what they might like to buy, and what are the special purchase opportunities (such as a statue of the Eiffel Tower or toy British soldiers wearing busbys). Preemptively inform them about things they will not be allowed to buy. For example, our kids are not allowed to buy brand name toys when traveling because they can't spend their travel money on the same stuff they can get at home. Talk about a few of the tricks that people use to try to convince you to spend your money, like putting up "BARGAIN" signs, displaying lots of trinkets in the window, or approaching you on the street.

Kids need the freedom to spend their own money in their own way, including experiencing the joy of a good deal, the satisfaction of saving for something special, and the disappointment of money squandered. In advance, decide how much money each child will have to spend. Trip money might be special money that you give each child before each trip, either an equal amount for each child or an amount based on his or her age. You might allow each child to withdraw a set amount from his or her own savings account or you might encourage each child to put away some portion of their allowance for several months in anticipation of the trip. However you decide to handle budgeting, let it become a traditional part of how you prepare for each family adventure. You'll be amazed at how these budgeting skills can end up trickling into their day-to-day lives. Plus, your kids will have a more realistic expectation of the kinds of things they can acquire on the road and that usually leads to fewer meltdowns and frustrations.

Also decide in advance whether all of the trip money will be available on Day One or whether it becomes available on a per-day or a per-destination basis. If your child is old enough, create a spending record to go with your budget spreadsheet (see "Spending Record"). You can paste a copy of the spending record into your child's journal (see chapter seven) so that they can track spending as they go. A spending record in which kids need to convert between currencies and a set of axes for graphing their spending over time is included in our budget resources section at the end of this chapter.

TIE IT ALL TOGETHER

Now that you have done a lot of reading, watched some films, learned a few phrases, and mapped your route, ask your kids questions about what they expect to experience on their trip. Ask them what they really want to see and if there is anything that they really want to avoid. Referencing all the new things you've learned in preparation for your trip, lead them on a virtual journey through your proposed itinerary. Make sure to stress the things in which they've shown the most interest. You will be able to generate a huge amount of excitement for what your children will discover in new places. And, as you'll learn in the next chapter, that excitement will only be amplified as you move into the next phase of preparing for your travels: packing!

BUDGET RESOURCES

These budget resources give you ideas for helping your children learn a little on-the-road math by taking ownership of part of the travel budget. Maybe they can help plan the whole trip budget with the sample "Budget Spreadsheet for Advance Planning." Maybe they can record their own souvenir budget so that they can know what they have spent and how much they have left to spend using the "Spending Record."

- Try creating similar sheets that are customized to your own journey. Maybe your kids can map out just the entertainment budget in advance, or create one spending record per country.
- The graphing axes allow kids to track their spending over time and give you some ideas for helping kids visualize the patterns. You could also track and graph savings accumulation before the trip.
- Photocopy the pages and then tape them into the front or back of your kids' journals so they're easily available for reference and use.

SAMPLE BUDGET SPREADSHEET

		Sun	Mon	Tue	Wed	Thu	Fri	Sat	Total
Adults									
Lodging									
Food	Restaurants								
	Groceries								
	Snacks								
Transportation	Within town								
	Between towns								
Entertainment	Museums								
	Theater								
Other									
Total									
Kids									
Ice cream/snacks									
Souvenirs									
Rides/experiences									
Total									
Grand Total									

© familyontheloose.com

SPENDING RECORD

Date	Country	Purchase	Amount (local currency)	Exchange Rate	Amount USD	Remaining Funds

TRACK YOUR SPENDING

Funds

Date

Instructions

- Start with your total budget. Reduce the amount available each day, each time you spend money, or each week.
- Use a different color for each location.
- Identify big purchases with an arrow and an annotation.
- If you planned your budget in advance, use a grey pencil to sketch in your planned spending, perhaps $20 per city. Then use colored pencils to graph the actual spending and compare.

3 Packing It In

We have a mantra whenever we start packing for a new trip: less stuff, more fun. It might seem like a fairly lofty goal to swing a four-week trip across Europe with three kids and only a couple of light bags, but it's possible. And, it's worth it. When traveling with children, packing light is all the more essential because sooner or later the adults are likely to be carrying almost everything and still trying to hold junior's hand or follow a teenager into a souvenir shop.

Luggage brings on claustrophobia. Too much luggage will trap you in your own stuff and prevent you from riding the bus with confidence, walking a few blocks to the hotel, or even grabbing a pastry and a cup of coffee on the way to the train. Ideally, you'd travel with only a toothbrush and a change of underwear. You would be free to walk, ride a bus, wander in and out of the museum, run for the train, or stop for ice cream. Realistically, however, you'll probably want to change your clothes once in a while and maybe even get dressed up for dinner. There is a good middle ground, but be forewarned: it takes a lot more energy and planning to pack two adults and a kid or two into one backpack than into three suitcases.

You can simplify your packing by simplifying your trip. Going to multiple climate zones or adding gear-intensive experiences compounds the luggage problem even if you're traveling alone. With kids, too many climates or too much gear is even more overwhelming. Less is more. It's so much easier to stay tropical at the beach than to swing by the ski slopes on the way. Start with modest plans encompassing one climatic zone and pick adventures for which you can rent the gear on location.

WHAT TO PACK IT ALL IN

This is not a trivial question. Backpack or roll-aboard? One big bag or four smaller bags? Two-wheel or four-wheel? There's no perfect solution but weigh the trade-offs seriously before you go. Backpacks leave your hands free and are harder to steal but they are, well, on your back, which can be pretty tiring. Rolling suitcases are handy in the airport, but rolling over sand or cobblestones or up stairs is not really fun.

There are three basic kinds of luggage: rolling suitcases, backpacks, and duffle bags. In order to decide which will work best for your family, think a little about where you will be and how much you'll be moving your stuff around.

- How will we be getting to the hotel and over what surfaces?
- Will we be able to keep our bags in a secured environment all the time?
- Are we particularly worried about security anywhere: airport in a developing country, leaving bags at a guesthouse during an overnight excursion, leaving bags in a tent if camping?
- Are there any tricky terrain issues such as trekking to a remote camp in the Himalayas or renting an apartment in Venice?
- Do we want to squeeze in odd equipment such as snorkle gear or roller skates?
- Are we bringing a laptop or other electronics that need protection?
- How many times are we moving all our stuff versus just heading out on day trips?

Rolling Suitcases

Why did it take humans so long to figure out that putting wheels and extendable handles on heavy suitcases was a good idea? Seriously, remember when traveling meant hauling heavy bags through the airport by actually carrying them? For good reason, wheeled suitcases are the most popular suitcase choice. Watch the baggage claim carousel some day: one black, wheeled suitcase after another. However, bags do come in every size and color. In fact, you can often find the more outlandish colors and patterns on discount. Bargain! And fun and easy to pick out on the carousel.

There are two important things to keep in mind about wheeled suitcases: wheels only help where they can roll, and four wheels are better than two. Bags with two wheels need to be tipped over and then dragged along. It's easier than carrying them but you still have to have a little strength and stamina over any distance. Bags with four wheels cost more but they are virtually weightless when rolling. You don't have to tip them over; you just push them along like a compact shopping cart. You can even rest your carry-on on top of the suitcase and push the whole pile of stuff around with one hand. Better yet, your three- or four-year-old can push a whole mountain of stuff around on his own. He might even be able to ride on top. These sorts of suitcases can also make for some excellent entertainment on long layovers if you're creative and careful (think "suitcase bowling" or "boarding gate relay").

A few more things to keep in mind if you're considering using rolling suitcases:

- Remember, these suitcases can't go up and down stairs. If you rented a fourth floor walk-up, all the wheels in the world won't help you.

- Hard cases are better than soft cases for any situation where security is an issue. Locking luggage is handy; you can also buy extra locks if your luggage doesn't have a built-in lock. (Note that any good thief can get through any good luggage lock so think of them as a deterrent, rather than as a truly preventative measure.)

- Invest in quality. If you are planning on pulling luggage around for a long time or in challenging situations, make sure it has sturdy wheels and zippers. Broken luggage is a big bummer and potentially a very expensive headache. If the zipper rips out in London, you have to waste your travel time hunting around to buy (with a generally painful exchange rate) a new suitcase before you can get on the plane to come home.

- Bags that come compartmentalized are a bonus. We like to have a zippered flap in the middle so that two people can share the internal space in peace.

- An outside pocket can be nice for tucking in last-minute items, but when they bulge, they often become too fat for overhead compartments.

- Extendable suitcases are terrific. You always come home with more than you packed so it's handy to be able to unzip yourself an extra two inches of storage.

Backpacks

All that said, we still prefer backpacks for their ease of access, expandability, simplicity on uneven ground, and happy, hands-free lifestyle. Anything on wheels is a challenge on the cobblestones of medieval cities or on unpaved trails between towns. And if you choose a backpack, there is an added incentive to keep the contents small and light.

Getting a backpack that fits you is the most critical variable in backpack selection. Good travel and camping stores should have many to choose from and someone to help you get the correct fit. Waist belts are essential for comfortably carrying the weight on your hips instead of your shoulders, and internal frames provide the structure to fit your load to your back. There are different loading styles to choose from, such as top versus sided loaded. Aside from personal preference, the major consideration in loading style is whether you can access most items in the pack without having to unload the bulk of the contents.

There are special travel backpacks that have a zip-on outer day bag, convenient water bottle access, and steel cable running through the handle for locks. If you can live with such a small day bag, these are very convenient. If you attach your day bag to the back of your backpack, you need to be aware of the pickpocket potential. Don't leave your camera or your wallet way back there out of sight. Some packs also come with thin pockets on the inside (next to your back) for your wallet, passport, and small valuables. You can't access them easily—but neither can anybody else.

One backpack or two? When our kids were little, we generally crammed into one backpack. That left one person with their hands and back free for toting kids, carrying the day bag, or simply moving quickly when needed. However, since backpacks are custom fit, it can be tough for both parents to share the load over time. Also, as the kids grow, so do their clothes. For older kids or bigger families, the one-backpack system is pretty difficult. As the kids grow, they are less likely to get carried and more able to carry their own backpacks; it becomes more efficient to branch out to one pack per person.

Duffle Bags

For all their faults, there is something endearing about a big old duffle bag. You toss everything in, pull the zipper closed, and swing it onto your shoulder. There's nothing fussy about a duffle bag. Everything is just a big soup inside, but there's also very little to go wrong. If packed loosely, a duffle bag can become any shape you want it to be. It even makes a nice pillow. For carrying your stuff long distances, however, duffle bags are a drag. They offer little security and almost no physical protection for your stuff. But a two-year-old can pack it! And strange-shaped objects can fit inside. If you're

BUDGET TIP

If your luggage fits in the overhead compartment and if you aren't exceeding your carry-on allowance, you can often check a carry-on bag at the gate for free. Airline staff are usually more than happy to check your bag early at the gate rather than waste time at the last minute with luggage that doesn't fit on board. The bags usually go all the way through to your final destination so you don't even have to drag them around on your layovers. Why would airlines offer this service? Since airlines started charging for checked baggage, everyone is carrying small suitcases on board and there simply isn't room for everything.

heading out for a long car trip or bringing a posse of teenage boys, don't rule out a cheap ol' duffle bag too quickly.

HOW BIG OF A BAG?

Whatever packing vessel you choose, you still have to decide on size. Carry-on dimensions vary by airline, so check their websites before heading to the airport (or luggage store). Since most airlines charge fees for checked baggage, it's really nice to have luggage that fits in the overhead compartments. However, given all the restrictions on liquids, it can also be necessary to have a designated checked bag. This might be the largest bag, with firm sides. Everyone's toiletries go into that one bag (in resealable plastic bags, of course).

Airlines also have weight limits on luggage, where exceeding the limit can sometimes result in extreme fees. Smaller luggage can help reduce the possibility of these fees, but efficient packing even in smaller bags can push the limit. Several times we've had to move items between bags while at the airport to avoid fees.

LEAVE IT AT HOME

Instead of focusing on what to bring, it may be easier to discuss what not to bring. Too much stuff will eventually paralyze you and your family—carrying it, storing it, safeguarding it. Everyone in the family has to buy into the "less stuff, more fun" philosophy. It simply won't work if three of you take the bare minimum and one of you brings the closet. Here are our three cardinal rules about what not to pack:

- Don't bring bulky stuff just because it's what you already own. Consider investing in some travel-centric gear. It is absolutely cost-effective to buy a few compressible rain jackets in order to avoid checking a huge suitcase containing a family of heavy plastic slickers and full-size umbrellas.
- Don't bring valuables. Kids are valuable and it's hard enough keeping

FASHION TIP: SMALL ACCESSORIES

If you feel the need to be stylish (or at least want to attempt it), pack small accessories. Five silk scarves will help you stay warm, dress up every outfit, and pack into a tiny ball that tucks into the corner of your suitcase. A cool necklace, fun socks, or an earring wardrobe in a divided plastic pill box are light and easy items that add spice to a basic travel wardrobe of simple tops and pants without adding weight or volume. Buying accessories on the road is a great system for bringing home practical souvenirs.

track of them. If you plan to dress up one evening, bring rhinestones. If you
need a laptop, don't bring a fancy one. It's liberating not to care about your stuff.

- Don't bring exciting fashion items. Bring basics that can mix and match. Inter-
changeable shirts and pants can provide more outfits for less size and weight.

Travel Clothes

You may want to invest in "travel clothes." Travel clothes do not wrinkle or are pat-
terned (to hide creases and dirt) so that they look better right out of the backpack.
You could also coordinate the color of the outfits of the people in your family, but
unless you want to look like a package tour group, we would not recommend
it. Once as we were walking down a street in Rome, Bill looked over his shoulder to see that our entire family of four was inadvertently wearing orange and
khaki. Oops! If you are more chic than we are (which is a pretty low bar actually),
you can find some pretty nice clothes made of fabric that wads up into a small
ball. The salespeople aren't thrilled when you shop by removing clothes from the
hanger and scrunching them up, but give it a try. Your kids' clothes will need to
have the same "scrunch-ability" as well as mix and match simplicity. For those of
you with simple tastes and low budgets, polyester Hawaiian shirts from Goodwill
are pretty scrunchable too.

No matter how short your trip, you shouldn't bring a different outfit for each
day. Don't bring six t-shirts when two will work just as well. Resign yourself to the
fact that laundry on the road is easier than carrying all those extra clothes. If you
bring clothes made from fast-drying materials, they can often be dry the morning
after washing them before bed. A little detergent from a prepacked travel bottle in
the bathroom sink, your polyester undies, a clothesline across the tub, and you're
good to go. Washing in the sink is annoying, but dragging around a big suitcase
is more so.

With all this stuff we're saying not to bring, what if you really need something
and you don't have it? If you forgot some vital part of your wardrobe at home, or it
wore out from overuse, or you lost it along the way somewhere, you can probably
replace it on the road. Sure, you may not find the exact thing that you are looking
for, but if you are flexible, shopping for it can be an adventure unto itself. Instead
of just strolling aimlessly through the weekend market, now you can find the kid
underwear section and haggle over a price!

One of our friends buys used clothes before he goes on a trip and discards
them as they wear out or get dirty. This means that the pack gets lighter as the
trip goes on. It also means that there is more room in there for the things he accu-
mulates along the way. Bringing clothes you plan to discard or give away can be

a lot of fun too. Bill left a "Manny, Moe, and Jack" t-shirt on the back of a kid in a remote village in India. We often wonder where it is now.

Lastly, accept reality. There are a few occasions when you just can't pack light. If you are packing for trekking the Pyrenees, eating an elegant Parisian dinner, and dancing at a Viennese ball, then no amount of efficient packing is going to make your luggage light and easy to carry. Whatever the reality, see the "Packing Checklist for Adults" at the end of this chapter.

PACKING FOR KIDS

Get your kids to commit to packing light. Just one too-big bag could mean you end up paying for checked luggage and then standing around waiting for it. More luggage also cramps that late-night taxi ride to the hotel from the airport. You must wait for, move, and keep track of the bags. Kids will follow your lead so talk out loud as you pack or have them help you pack first in order to get them on board with traveling light.

One way we've limited what everyone can bring is by providing each person with a packing cube or stuff sack. Make allowances for body size in the size of the stuff sack. Dad's clothes will need more space than your son's clothes and the six-year-old will need more space than the three-year-old, even if they're packing the exact same number of outfits. Make it a challenge: "Can you fit all the clothes you need into this little sack?" In each hotel room, you can pass out the small inner bags and then collect them again in the morning.

Let your kids pack themselves! Give them a list with check boxes, a colored pencil, and set them loose (see "Packing Checklist for Kids" and "Packing List for Emerging Readers" at the end of this chapter). If you let your kids pick out their favorite clothes and accessories, it will greatly reduce the quibbling about what to wear once you're on the road. Set the parameters up front: is it or is it not okay to bring a princess dress or superhero costume on the trip? Pack early so you can stay calm and oversee the process. Bigger kids can handle more packing responsibility and they will have some serious incentive to pack light since they'll probably have to carry their own stuff. If your child swears he will be fine carrying the fifty pound backpack full of books, let him give it a try: pack it all up and then give it a test-drive by carrying it around the block, to the playground, and to the grocery store for a shopping expedition. If he's still okay, then maybe he's right. But more likely, he'll decide to jettison some of the less essential items.

After making a pile of everything they plan to bring, have the kids set aside one plane outfit—from undies to sneakers. Then they can pack the rest of their gear into the stuff sack or suitcase.

SAVE SPACE

Make sure everyone saves a little free space in his or her pack or suitcase. You will accumulate stuff as you go. We don't understand why or how it happens, or, more importantly, why we can't seem to prevent it, but our kids' backpacks fill up with junk at an alarmingly fast rate. Brochures, a box of unfinished candy, a small toy, the comic book in Japanese for a friend back home who loves anime, the free trinket that came with their soda pop, the cool plastic gelato bowl, and the free gift from the well-meaning man at the market—it all adds up. We suggest bringing a mini "stuff" sack for each kid's backpack. When the sack is full, that's it. Ship it home if it's really so valuable you must have it or if you have a long trip. Or take a photo of it and leave it there.

SPECIAL TRAVEL GEAR WORTH CONSIDERING

There is no need to buy out the store, but there may be a few items that could make your life easier on the road. You can usually get everything with one swing through an outdoor supply store and another through the drugstore. Some of our favorite special items include:

Walking shoes: On trips where you will be relying on your feet as a major mode of travel, you can never overestimate the importance of good shoes. Be sure to break them in before you go and consider special insoles for added support.

Luggage: As we discussed, whether it's a wheeled suitcase, a backpack, or a duffle bag, choose what's right for you and be mindful of size, weight, and quality. Since you may develop a strong attachment to the right bag over time, it's worth a significant investment.

Travel clothes: Some clothes are lighter, tougher, don't wrinkle, and don't show dirt as much as others. Quick-drying fabrics will be dry in the morning after being washed out the night before (in other words, it's possible to go with only two pairs of underwear per person). Coordinating the colors of clothes allows more combinations with fewer items.

Packing cubes/Stuff sacks: These are small compressible bags, usually with at least one mesh face and a nice strong zipper. You can squeeze a lot of stuff in and zip it up to maximize space. Packing cubes can keep your luggage organized, and each person can be responsible for unpacking and repacking his own cube at each stop. They are also good for segregating dirty laundry. Note that these only reduce volume, not weight, so be cautious in how you use them.

Hanging toiletry bags: These are expensive but nifty. Make sure that there is a secure section for liquids so that if they leak during pressurized air travel, your other things don't get sticky. If you plan to carry your luggage on, have a system that makes it easy to get your liquids out at security.

Travel-size toiletries: The small bottles of shampoo and conditioner you collect from hotels are great for using in places that don't supply them for free. Deodorant and toothpaste also come in small travel sizes, though we are constantly surprised at how quickly a family can go through a tiny tube of toothpaste. If you want to stick with your favorite toiletry brands, you can transfer them from their original large containers into smaller refillable ones. But be careful of cheapo plastic bottles that tend to crack and break easily.

First-aid kit: You can get a prepacked kit at most pharmacies or outdoor stores, but you may be better off customizing it to your personal needs by putting it together yourself (see "First-Aid Kit Ingredients" later in this chapter).

Resealable plastic bags: These come in many sizes. They are great for compartmentalizing and protecting the smaller stuff. Freezer strength bags will hold more and last longer. Bring extra resealable plastic bags—and then pack a few more resealable plastic bags. You can never have too many.

Travel-size water bottles: Make sure they are light, unbreakable, and have a tight seal. They have to be empty only when going through airport security. If you're going somewhere where you don't trust the water, see your local camping store for several lightweight water treatment options.

Compact windbreakers: Windbreakers that fit into a little stuff sack are particularly easy to manage and can act as short-term rain protection. When combined with a fleece jacket they can also provide impressive warmth.

Ultra-light umbrellas: These are for those days when the windbreaker isn't going to cut it as protection from the storm. This is one of those items we tend to intentionally leave at home and accumulate on the road when we need it, hedging our hopeful bets that the weather will stay nice. They can be found readily and cheaply in most cities when it rains, and unfortunately we now have a nice collection. They also can provide shade on really hot days.

Kids can still pick up small souvenirs and postcards. They can also take photos, write notes, or draw what they see. (We provide lots of ideas for journaling in chapter seven). Keeping them busy on creating memories instead of shopping is cost effective. But be honest to your original budget plan: if they can afford it on their budget, let them make their own choice. If they find the coolest sweater in the world, a unique pair of shoes they've never seen before, a stuffed animal, or a painting they absolutely have to have, make them add shipping to the cost of the item and then, if it's within their budget, buy it and ship it straight home.

THE DAY BAG

You will need at least one little bag that is easy to carry around and comfortable whether it has a little or a lot of stuff in it. The day bag will accompany you on any day trips you take away from your hotel or other home base. It should be big enough for camera, weather gear (collapsible umbrella, hat, and rain or fleece jacket), small snack, micro first-aid kit (see upcoming sections "Medical Mishaps" and "The First Aid Kit"), wallet, cell phone, and map. For infants and toddlers, throw in a sealed plastic bag with a change of clothes (compacted by squeezing the air out), the diaper kit, and bottles if needed. You may also want to include books, crayons, and journals to help you get through waiting times. The bag should be small enough that it never weighs you down. Don't start out in the

WHAT GOES IN THE DAY BAG?
Basics include:
- ☐ Wallet/cash
- ☐ Camera
- ☐ Water
- ☐ Mini first-aid kit
- ☐ Hats (for shade if it's hot and for warmth if it's cold)
- ☐ Jackets (stuffable, rain-resistant windbreakers)
- ☐ Tissues
- ☐ Snacks (fruit, energy bars, etc.)
- ☐ Diapers/wipes
- ☐ Change of clothes (for the toddling travelers)

Other items frequently found in a well-stocked day bag: sunscreen, sunglasses, gloves, small umbrella, passports, wipes (even if no one is in diapers anymore), journals or journaling supplies, map, guidebook, phone, and tiny entertainment (tiny markers, small book, deck of cards, bubbles, etc.).

morning with the day bag full because you never know what snacks, souvenirs, or other "treasures" you will find during the day. Stuffing these items in your day bag will be much easier than carrying around a shopping bag.

We like bags that have outer straps and loops that are designed for dangling sweaters or jackets. If you can carry these items on the outside, you won't need to reserve space for them on the inside. The bag also has to be comfy to carry. Ashley likes a bag with one fat strap (more like a big purse) that can go over one shoulder or diagonally across neck and shoulder. Bill likes a medium-sized bag that can be worn as a fanny pack or with a shoulder strap. Day bags that can be carried in two ways give you options.

Many people like backpacks but we haven't had success with them as day bags. First, all your stuff is behind you. You can't just zip it open and grab a snack or the

ELECTRONICS

There is something liberating (or maybe just self-righteous) about traveling electronics-free, but this is the twenty-first century and few folks can do it. Some electronics that can save space and entertain kids include:

Smart phones: These can function as a map (download these ahead at home), a camera, a GPS device (for a price), a phone (for a price), a personal music player, or a laptop (free where there is wireless).

Tablets: iPads and similar tablets can store addresses, books, educational activities, movies, maps, journals, photos, and more. You can also use them to Skype with friends or family back home.

eBook readers: Kindles and similar e-readers can save a lot of weight in books, especially if your kids love reading or you're on a long trip. Remember though that browsing local bookstores is pretty great too and used English-language books often fetch a nice trade-in price.

Hand-held games: Although Nintendo DS and similar games can provide hours and hours of entertainment, they are frequently overused. It's really sad (and a little embarrassing) to see American kids playing Mario Kart in a European cathedral. So think carefully before bringing something like this along. You may need to set very clear rules about its use (for example, only on the airplane).

Overall, think it through and be efficient. Minimize your valuables and maximize your kids' connection to the trip itself.

camera. You have to take off one strap, flip the bag around, fish your stuff out, and then put it back on. Or you have to ask your partner repeatedly "Can you get the ____ out of the pack for me?" Also, backpacks tend to bang into other people and get stuck in bus doors. Lastly, in a crowd, you can't easily hug your bag close to protect it. Your stuff is just back there for anyone to unzip. Along the same lines, it's a good idea for your day bag to have a safe pocket for your valuables that can't be reached eas-ily by strangers. You'll also appreciate an easy-access pocket for snacks and other nonvaluables and an outside pocket for the water bottle. This day bag might double as your carry-on for the plane.

One day bag or two? We prefer two slightly smaller bags. Why? First off, marital bliss. Carrying your own stuff means less griping and fewer wasted words. "It's your turn to carry the bag" gets dull. Also, each bag is lighter if you're carrying two. Build in some cross-bag redundancy. When you are separated, you'll both still have the basic resources. It's nice for each parent to be able to grab a kid or two and go.

So why not have the kids carry their own stuff? More day bags could equal more fun, right? Well, it has never worked for us. In the airport or on a train, when all you are doing is getting from here to there with your stuff, a bag for every family member gives the kids some independence and responsibility for their own entertainment. But daily adventures and sightseeing is a whole different ball of wax. On the bus, into the café, back on the street, into the museum bag-check, back on the street, into the playground, onto the tram, onto the bus, down the trail, into the shop, back to the hotel, and then to dinner. Trust us, no matter what system you started with, you are going to end up with lost bags, adults car-rying all the bags, or both.

PACKING FOR THE UNEXPECTED

Obviously you can't plan or pack for every contingency, but you can at least be prepared for the unexpected. Accept that the trip won't go exactly as you expect, and pack accordingly. Flight delays, lost luggage, weather, and illness are the biggies but there are plenty of other quirky surprises.

Surprise Travel "Opportunities"

Heavily booked flights and foul weather can cause delays or cancellations, but these unexpected changes in itinerary don't have to be all bad. Be mentally and physically prepared for last-minute changes. Airport time can be family time, if you stash a few fun items in your carry-on such as crayons or playing cards. (We'll give you lots of additional ideas for airport games in chapter four.) Keep a few basics in your carry-on bags to get you through unexpected overnights: a change of underwear, a toothbrush, daily medications, and some extra diapers. These small additions will also come in super handy in the event of lost luggage. We had two days in Spain

THE PACKING TIMELINE

☐ Find out what the carry-on size and weight restrictions are for your airline.

☐ Determine what arrangement of suitcases, carry-ons, and day bags you'll bring.

☐ Make the packing lists (for adults and children).

☐ Purchase any items you need (clothing, first-aid, plane gifts, etc.).

☐ Pile up all the stuff and go through it. Remove the items you can live without.

☐ Set out the plane outfit(s).

☐ Pack the first-aid and micro first-aid kits.

☐ Pack your suitcases/duffles.

☐ Pack your carry-on bags (see chapter four).

☐ Wrap and pack plane gifts and snacks (see chapter four).

without our bags. We converted some extra plastic bags into baby bottle liners and took the opportunity to visit the local market first thing in the morning. We found a cheap change of clothes and had a great introduction to Spanish life.

Wacky Weather

Of course the weather can be unpredictable. We've had 100 degree days in Paris, August snow in Montana, and daily monsoon rains in Thailand. Bring at least one warm item and one cool item everywhere, every season. Expecting warm weather in Hawaii in June and bringing only shorts is just begging for a freak storm. Hats and jackets can be versatile for sun, cold, and rain. Bringing a fleece jacket and a thin rain/wind jacket is better than bringing one insulated jacket as you'll have more options. Our kids each have a black fleece jacket that they bring everywhere. If it is a little chillier, they can add a warm hat. They also have a windbreaker shell that packs down into a little sack. This combination can be modified to fit most mid-range weather. Don't even think about packing an extra fleece (just in case) or an extra pair of mittens or a heavier raincoat. If you are really frozen or soggy, you can most likely buy something wherever you are.

Snack Attacks

Packing a few familiar emergency snacks is wise. Familiar snacks can help avoid the short tempers that come with low blood sugar. Dried fruit, microwavable macaroni and cheese, or anything small and storable that both you and your kids will eat in a pinch are worth their weight in gold. Keep snacks hidden from your kids to reduce begging. Some restocking of snacks is usually possible along the way, so there is no need to bring a lot.

Money Mix-ups

Pack a little cash, even in these days of credit cards and ATMs. There can be random business closures from holidays that you've never heard of. Ashley once arrived in Paris with no cash on a bank holiday. Thankfully, she had a trusting cab driver. She also got stuck in Korea, unable to pay for lodging, on a bank holiday in which even the ATMs couldn't be accessed. It happens!

Medical Mishaps

Chances are that at some point during your trip, one of you won't be feeling well. Even though being sick or injured is no fun for anyone, it could be an opportunity to slow way down and explore the television channels, enjoy a book in the shade, or experiment with siestas. Allowing enough recuperation time is hard when you think about what you've invested in the trip, but be patient and get healthy. Watching local people from a park bench as your kids enjoy a playground can be both fascinating and recuperative.

THE FIRST AID KIT

Bringing the necessary supplies to deal with minor health crises as they arise is critical. A well-stocked first-aid kit is an absolute necessity. In our list of kit ingredients (see "First-Aid Kit Ingredients") we detail the types of medications and first-aid equipment that you may want to include. Use some common sense, however: you do not need to bring a complete kit on a weekend trip to Vancouver, B.C., and there may be a few more things you require for a three-month trek across the Himalayas. If there is an item that no one in your family has ever needed and you cannot see why travel would change that fact, do not bring it along. The list is meant only as a guide.

There are many ways to shrink the weight and volume of your first-aid kit without sacrificing completeness. First, consider whether you need a giant supply or a small supply. Many medications can be purchased (though often for an exaggerated cost) in small, single dose packaging. Check several local drugstore chains and adventure/outdoor stores for single-dose packages. Sometimes, pre-packaged first-aid kits can be a great source of these convenient items, even if you do not use everything included (unused items can be stashed away for use in a car first-aid kit at home). You can remove most medications from their larger cardboard packaging, but be careful to retain the instructions for their use. Tape those instructions to the bottle or to the sheet of pills. Naturally, make sure your kids do not have ready access to your prescription and over-the-counter drugs, many of which look invitingly like candy. We carry our medications in a nontransparent cosmetic bag, fixed with a small luggage lock.

Actually, we carry three first-aid kits! All medications are in the small, locked cosmetic bag. We also have a small, heavy-duty, resealable plastic bag (designed to carry hiking maps and available from outdoor stores) filled with physical first-aid items (band-aids, gauze, etc.). Keeping these items in two separate packages makes them easier to pack. Lastly, we carry a micro first-aid kit—an "ouch pouch"—in our day bag to address skinned knees and headaches. It's smaller than either of our wallets and it's the one we use the most, so restocking it after a rough day is necessary. Note that if you have special health concerns such as allergies, you may need to carry a few extra items in your day bag.

A Few Last Things

Packing is the finale of the travel preparations. Although we've said a lot about what *not* to bring, the most important guideline is to keep the "pack light" philosophy at the forefront of your mind as you decide what you'll really need and how to carry it most comfortably.

The end of this chapter marks the end of the "Ready, Set ..." section of the book. Hopefully, you're feeling both "ready" and "set" to lead your family through the preparation phase of an amazing travel adventure. In the next section, we begin the journey itself: "...Go!"

FIRST-AID KIT INGREDIENTS

Medications

Go over these with your physician so you know when to use each medicine and how much to give each family member.

☐ Aspirin (adults)
☐ Ibuprofen (adults)*
☐ Acetaminophen (adults)
☐ Ibuprofen (children or infant)
☐ Acetaminophen (children or infant)
☐ Antacid*
☐ Antidiarrheal
☐ Laxative
☐ Hemorrhoid suppositories
☐ 3 in 1 antibacterial ointment*
☐ Decongestant
☐ Antinausea (adults)
☐ Travel sickness prophylactic
☐ Antihistamine (oral)
☐ Antihistamine (external applicator for bug bites)
☐ Diaper rash medication (infants)
☐ Ear infection numbing drops (small kids)
☐ Antifungal cream
☐ Hydrocortisone cream*
☐ Digital, plastic thermometer
☐ Syrup of ipecac (ask your doctor if he/she recommends)
☐ Urinary tract infection numbing meds (if a frequent problem)
☐ Yeast infection medication (if a frequent problem)
☐ Canker sore/herpes medication (if a frequent problem)
☐ Prescription antibiotic (adult and child doses)
☐ Prescriptions for your family's unique needs (bring extra in case of spills)

First-Aid Supplies

☐ Antiseptic wipes*
☐ Iodine (for drinking water)
☐ Band-aids (all sizes and shapes—and characters)*
☐ Sterile gauze
☐ Moleskin (to treat or prevent blisters)*
☐ Ace bandage
☐ Waterproof tape
☐ Portable splint (EZ Splint)
☐ Instant ice pack
☐ Small dull scissors
☐ Tweezers
☐ Maxi-pads (useful for bandaging wounds)*

Many items can be found in single-dose packaging; starred* items are useful to carry in your micro first-aid kit.

The following packing lists can be photocopied and given to your kids to help them remember everything that they need to bring.

- Talk with your kids about the list, so they know how they can use it and what you expect them to do. Walk the nonreaders through the list, explaining what you need them to pack for each picture.
- Write in any specialty items that your kids should bring to meet their own particular needs or the needs of a particular trip.
- At first, it's probably a good idea to go through the pile of stuff and the list with each child to make sure that everything (and not too much extra) is there.
- If you discover that you've forgot something important on the trip, add it onto the packing list so you don't forget it again the next trip.

PACKING CHECKLIST FOR ADULTS

- ☐ T-shirts
- ☐ Dress shirts
- ☐ Shorts
- ☐ Long pants
- ☐ Underwear (quick-drying)
- ☐ Socks
- ☐ Nice outfit
- ☐ Accessories
- ☐ Jacket (water repellent)
- ☐ Warm sweater or thin jacket (that can fit under the water repellent jacket)
- ☐ Bathing suit
- ☐ Sunscreen
- ☐ Small flashlight
- ☐ Toiletries (small bag/case)
- ☐ Walking shoes
- ☐ Special shoes (water shoes/flip flops, boots, dressy shoes, etc.)
- ☐ First-aid kit
- ☐ Water bottle
- ☐ Camera
- ☐ Passports and paperwork
- ☐ Guidebooks
- ☐ Sun/rain hat
- ☐ Collapsible umbrella
- ☐ Books/eBook reader
- ☐ Cell phone
- ☐ Power cords for all electronics (phone, eBook reader, laptop, etc.)
- ☐ Power outlet adapters if necessary

If Traveling with Babies

- ☐ Diapers
- ☐ Wipes
- ☐ Small diaper changing kit
- ☐ Baby food
- ☐ Formula
- ☐ Gadgets (sling, cloth high-chair, walking harness, etc.)

Packing List for Kids

Short-sleeved shirt ☐ ☐ ☐

Long-sleeved shirt ☐ ☐ ☐

Pants ☐ ☐

Shorts ☐

Underpants ☐ ☐ ☐ ☐ ☐ ☐

Socks ☐ ☐ ☐ ☐ ☐ ☐

Nice outfit ☐

Bathing suit ☐

Toothbrush ☐

Toothpaste ☐

Hairbrush ☐

Hair bands or clips ☐ ☐ ☐ ☐

Pajamas ☐

Small stuffed animal or favorite toy ☐

Book or eBook ☐

Rain jacket ☐

Fleece jacket ☐

Walking shoes ☐

Special shoes for water, snow, or nice outfit ☐

Hat ☐

Do you have special toiletries that you need (medication, retainer, etc.)?

_____ ☐

_____ ☐

Packing List for the Emerging Reader

short-sleeved shirt

long-sleeved shirt

pants

shorts

underpants

socks

nice outfit

pajamas

toothbrush

toothpaste

hairbrush

hair bands or clips

small stuffed animal

book or eBook

rain jacket

fleece jacket

walking shoes

special shoes

hat

Part 2
Go!

Go!

To travel hopefully is a better thing than to arrive.
—*Robert Louis Stevenson*

You are embarking on a family adventure! And in the true family spirit, everyone wants to do something different: you want to see the iconic paintings in the local museum and sip wine at a quiet restaurant, junior wants to eat ice cream and swing on the playground, and your spouse has grand ideas about hiking in a national park. Don't fret! While these aspirations may seem to be at odds, you can balance it all by ratcheting back your expectations and not clinging to a stereotypical tourist's fourteen-hour daily tour schedule. After all, you and your family are not stereotypical tourists. Start by reminding yourself that you do not need to do or see every single thing mentioned in the guidebook or sample the fare in every possible restaurant. The goal is to have the best day possible every day, and that likely will not include a dawn-to-dusk tour. Ask yourself, do you really want to plod into one more gallery? Be thankful for the excuse to take a slower pace. Kids give you a reason to hang out at the Parisian café and eat crepes all morning! A relaxed pace is a smart decision for the kids, and a great opportunity for you. If missing out on an experience or two rankles a bit, we have a mantra that always helps: "We will be back someday!"

In this section of the book, we focus on the trip itself. In chapter four, we talk about surviving, and maybe even enjoying, the long flight from home. We include lists of activities that you and your kids can use to pass the time in the airport and on the plane. Chapter five delves into creating daily routines and adventures so that your kids will know what is expected of them on the road. We provide loads of ideas for what to do with those 15 minutes before the bus comes and how to enjoy dinner in a quiet restaurant with your entire family in tow. Chapter six describes creative ways to inject education into your trip, helping you and your kids add depth to the adventure. We cover museum scavenger hunts, ecological hikes, historic timelines, and more. Lastly, in chapter seven, we get crazy with journaling. There are ideas for keeping track of your activities, writing stories, observing local culture, making maps, sketching plants, and interviewing each other—just to name a few. Don't worry. The kids won't know any of this is good for them. Just buckle up and let these ideas turbo-boost your adventure.

4 Taking Flight

T he hardest part of your trip is now behind you—you have planned, prepared, packed, and walked out the door! You're ready for the next phase of your adventure, but few look forward to a long train, plane, or bus ride. Most people outside of business class view time on a plane—with cramped leg room, the seat in front of you reclining into your face, and bad food (if any)—as survival territory. With kids, the venture can be even more daunting. But wait! Plane travel can actually be fun!

This chapter describes how to have fun on a long plane ride—or, at the very least, make it a more tolerable part of your journey. We describe what to pack in your carry-ons, how to entertain your kids at the airport, and ideas for in-flight amusement. We also explain the benefits of getting bumped from overbooked flights, how to finesse your checked and carry-on bags, and the best way to make your strollers, port-a-cribs, and carseats someone else's burden.

As always, preparation is the key. To make a long flight successful, prepare the kids' expectations and the carry-ons. Given all the preparation you've done prior to departure day, the kids should be pretty excited. They helped you plan the trip, carefully packed their stuff, and have a general idea of the itinerary. They may even be too restless to sleep the night before departure. While the final goal for the day is to get where you are going safe and sound, your objective along the way is to keep the kids involved in things that they enjoy so that they do not have time to get bored and cranky. It takes a little extra energy to prevent meltdowns, but it's well worth it.

Keep Kids Informed of the Travel Schedule

When kids know exactly what is coming down the pike, everything runs smoother.

Sketch the plan out for them as best you can. You might even type it out and let them have a copy. For example:

1. We are leaving at eight a.m. on Friday.
2. Aunt Mabel will drive us to the airport.
3. We will each carry our own carry-on bag.
4. Our flight will be eight hours long, but broken into two parts.
5. We will switch planes in Detroit with no time for browsing. We may have to run to catch the second flight.
6. We will eat lunch on the plane and I will bring snacks.
7. There might be movies to watch and I have a few surprises for you.
8. When we land, we will be in _____!
9. Tonight we'll be sleeping in _____!

Allow for a lot of extra time. There is no reason to squeeze in an extra twenty minutes of sleep only to be rushed and anxious at the airport. Plan to arrive with plenty of time to spare, so you can enjoy a cup of coffee or play some airport games (see "Twelve Active Activities for the Airport"). Everyone will appreciate a little transition time between each phase of your journey.

Be Flexible with Travel and Sleeping Attire

Pajamas can be excellent travel clothing. For late flights, why not travel in pajamas? If your kids are walking, we don't recommend footie pajamas because airport floors are filthy. Mid-weight pajamas can be stylish with sneakers or sandals and nightgowns can be paired with those party shoes that are tricky to fit in the suitcase. Once on board, kids can kick off their shoes and be ready for sleep. On long flights that go from afternoon into nighttime, you can change them into pajamas, brush teeth, and have a bedtime story in-flight. Familiar bedtime rituals in the air might help kids get to sleep a little faster.

If you have a very early flight, put your kids to bed the night before in their travel clothes. Pack a portable breakfast of yogurt, precut fruit, a breakfast bar, or a bagel with cream cheese, with a juice box and a napkin in a brown paper bag. In the morning, just wake them up by carrying them out to the car. After you strap them into the car, pass them their brown bag breakfast and hit the road. They'll love it!

Be Prepared with "Plane Gifts"

Plane gifts can be anything that your child may find interesting or engaging, such as cards, puzzles, small toys, coloring books, or other craft projects (see the "Ten Ideas for Plane Gifts" boxes for various ages). Avoid toys with tiny parts as they will inevitably disappear between the seats or fall into the aisle just as the flight attendants are serving drinks. Messy, spillable, heavy, active, noisy, and big things are no fun. Small stuffed animals and inflatable pillows are okay, but they are space hogs for the ninety seven percent of the time that you are not using them. Places to look for little gifts include the "impulse buy" racks near cash registers at toy stores, bookstores, and drugstores. Party stores are excellent for cheap party favors that are fun and relatively disposable. But to find the best, longest-lasting toys, simply keep an eye out whenever you are shopping. Buy good gifts when you find them and tuck them in a travel box in the closet. The buy-early system will increase the diversity of gifts your children can discover in-flight and will give you one less thing on your last minute "to do" list.

Our strategy is to wrap the new items as gifts and dole them out slowly during the flight. The wrapping heightens anticipation, and unwrapping takes an extra two minutes of plane time (it all adds up!). Sometimes we carry all the gifts and

TEN IDEAS FOR PLANE GIFTS: UNDER THREE YEARS OLD

1. Crayola Color Wonder markers and paper.
2. Stickers and a sticker book with slick pages so you can reuse the stickers later.
3. A roll of masking tape to make sticky loops to entertain infants or to paste together pictures from the in-flight magazine.
4. A sheet of felt and a bunch of homemade felt shapes.
5. A cluster of silver, hinged notebook rings. These can be linked to nearly anything so they won't get dropped. They make a pleasing tinkling sound but they're not too noisy. These are available at office supply stores.
6. Simple hand or finger puppets.
7. Plastic spoons or stacking cups.
8. Plastic slinky.
9. Fat, flexible, corregated plastic tube. They sell these as toys that can be collapsed and stretched; you can also purchase a length of this tubing from a home improvement store in the plumbing section. Hold one end up to the air vent and then shoot the air anywhere you want from the other end, or you can whisper through it across seats. Just fiddling with it is fun too!
10. Animal, insect, or cartoon cards. These are sold in lots of toy stores and even many drugstores. They can be sorted, inspected, spread out, piled up, and turned into guessing games or story characters.

TEN IDEAS FOR PLANE GIFTS: THREE-TO-SIX YEARS OLD

1. Stickers and a sticker book with slick pages so you can reuse the stickers later.
2. Coloring book with a very small set of markers (useful for restaurants later).
3. Little cars or dolls.
4. A bag of colored pipe cleaners to make glasses, dolls, bikes, cars, shape mobiles, and more.
5. Small books of stickers, stencils, mazes, etc. (Dover Publishers produces these for usually $1–$2 each), and a set of colored pencils.
6. Tiny story books. Annikin Press produces over twenty-five titles with complete stories and full color drawings for $1.50 each. These books measure about two square inches and we love them.
7. Decks of cards (not necessarily playing cards—number cards, animal cards, vehicle cards, and so on).
8. Sewing cards (these can be homemade).
9. Paper bags and markers to make puppets.
10. Magnetic sets. Regular magnets work fine and are fun if they don't fall apart too easily and get lost between the seats; some play magnets come in tins that can be decorated.

keep them hidden until we dole them out. Sometimes we give each kid a little pile of wrapped presents to carry and we put them in control of timing when they can open the next gift. Be careful that plane gifts are opened slowly enough that there is still something left for the second half of the flight. Wait to give them a new gift until they have exhausted their interest in the last one. By the early teenage years, they should be able to coordinate their own entertainment (though even teens appreciate an in-flight surprise!). If you are feeling really clever, pack a few extra wrapped gifts in your checked luggage for the flight home or pick some up as you travel.

WHAT TO BRING ON THE PLANE

Each family member should have one carry-on bag. Airlines are becoming stricter every day at enforcing size limitations for carry-on bags so use their guidelines to limit yourself. You don't want to be carrying around big heavy bags anyway. If you decide to bring only carry-on baggage on your trip, organize it so that the items

TEN IDEAS FOR PLANE GIFTS: SIX TO NINE YEARS OLD

1. Comic books or tiny story books. Check used bookstores.
2. Mini-puzzles, especially three-dimensional mini-puzzles.
3. Modeling clay in assorted colors.
4. Mad Libs.
5. Simple craft kits, such as yarn and a crochet hook or a finger knitter. Look for tiny craft kits as you shop in fabric or craft supply stores.
6. Travel activity books. Don't forget those invisible ink travel books—often cheaper when bought somewhere besides the airport!
7. ViewMasters can still be pretty cool. Don't forget to get extra slides.
8. Brain puzzlers such as miniature Rubik's cubes or small metal rings you have to figure out how to separate.
9. Small games you can play with your child like card games or dice games. The best ones have dice that are trapped inside something so they can't be lost. These will come in handy when you get to your destination, too. Minimize loose parts and bring replacements if possible.
10. Okay, okay. Small digital games are often cheap and always a kid-pleaser. Make sure they can be muted!

you'll need in-flight are easily accessible in their own separate container at the very top of the backpack or suitcase. Before you stow your bag in the overhead compartment, pull out this small sack of items and tuck it in your seat pocket or on the floor in front of you.

What about bringing a carseat on board? If your child has his or her own airplane seat and you're traveling with a carseat, by all means bring it on board. It gets strapped into the seat and then, wonderfully, your child gets strapped in too. Your child already expects not to be able to move around when they're strapped into a carseat so being unable to move around in-flight won't come as a surprise. Parents then have their hands free for entertaining or feeding kids—or even enjoying a snack themselves. The carseat will be familiar and easy to sleep in too. The only downside to bringing a carseat on board is that it is bulky to carry around in the airport. Consider a set of portable wheels, available in most luggage sections. Also note that if you're traveling with a child under two who doesn't have his own seat on board, you can ask at the gate whether there is likely to be an empty seat next to you. If the plane isn't too full and the airline staff member is helpful, he might even volunteer to move folks around to arrange for an empty seat beside you. If you do bring a carseat on board and there turns out to be no room for it, the flight attendant can check the carseat at the gate and it will be waiting for you next to the airplane door when you land.

If you're bringing a booster seat on your trip, check it! They're bulky and aren't helpful in flight. Checking carseats and booster seats does not currently count against your checked-luggage quota for any airline we're familiar with. Most airlines also offer huge sturdy plastic bags for checked baggage. You can ask for one at the counter and put any baby gear inside to prevent it from getting filthy and protect straps.

The Kid Carry-On

Kids' carry-on bags should be small and light enough for them to tote around easily. We like backpacks but the best bag for your kid is the bag they want to carry around. It is likely, of course, that you will be carrying their bags somewhere along the line too. Keeping their bags manageable from the start will minimize the amount of time you end up lugging around a pink poodle purse or a light-up Spiderman backpack.

The kids' bags should be devoted entirely to things that they will need or want on the plane (see "The Kids' Carry-On Checklist"). While older kids can usually carry their full complement of personal stuff, younger kids may only be able to pack their own entertainment. Be prepared to lug snacks, water, and extra clothes on their behalf.

In-flight entertainment needs to be small and light. It can include toys that the kids already know (and that you have confidence will keep them occupied for a while), or the plane gifts that you have stashed in one of your carry-ons. Another strategy is to use the now ubiquitous portable video games or DVD players. Though our preference is to exhaust our children's interest in creative gifts before resorting to digital games and movies, kids can undoubtedly spend lots of time playing video games and watching in-flight DVDs. The less you allow these activities at home, the longer they'll be interesting when you really need them. And electronic childcare will allow you some down time to read your own book

---

THE KIDS' CARRY-ON CHECKLIST

- ☐ Things to do—e-Reader or book, workbook, magazine, coloring book, plain paper, pens or pencils, favorite toy, music and portable video games with headphones, etc.
- ☐ Wrapped plane presents
- ☐ Special snacks or treats
- ☐ Empty water bottle (to be filled after going through security)
- ☐ A pair of warm socks
- ☐ A sweater or light jacket
- ☐ Cell phone (older kids)
- ☐ Wallet (older kids)

TRAVEL TIP: TAG TEDDY

How many teddy bears, favorite stuffed animals, or blankies have been left on board and lost forever? Too many! They slip between the seats when kids are sleeping, are tucked into unexpected places, or get missed during the hubub of gathering adult valuables and cranky kids at the end of a long flight. It's a tragedy you should do everything to avoid. Grab a luggage tag at check-in, fill it out, and attach it to the bear, rabbit, or blanket corner; use a safety pin if necessary. Even if you have already written your name and phone number on this item (which you should do!), the tag will get folks' attention. When you fill out the tag, add "Best Friend—Please Return" or some other note that will tug at the heart of even the grumpiest maintenance staff, include all your contact information. Hopefully, your child will be quickly reunited with her friend.

or take a nap. For the sanity of all involved, please make sure you bring head-phones for the video games or activate the mute button. If you are traveling with multiple children but only one DVD device, use an audio splitter to enable more than one headphone set; they can be purchased at most electronics stores for only a few dollars.

The Parent Carry-On

Your carry-on bag should house all the essentials that you can't risk being lost in your checked baggage: plane tickets, passports, prescription medications, money, reservation confirmations, and camera. It should also include the essentials for enjoying the plane flight: diapers, favorite snacks, drinking water, and your read-ing materials. For smaller children, be ready with lollipops, raisins, or another quick snack to relieve the ear pain associated with changes in air pressure during take-offs and landings. Older kids should do well with chewing gum.

We always carry enough with us to survive one night. You never know when planes will be delayed, luggage will be lost, or you will have the opportunity to get bumped. It's really not much to carry if you think *flexibility* and *survival*. Tiny toothbrushes and hairbrushes are easy to find in the travel section of drugstores, and disposable travel toothbrushes are often handed out on long flights. Save them for when you really need them! You can sleep in your travel shirt or even without pajamas altogether. Your kids will grow by discovering how little they really need and how creative and fun it can be to do without.

THE PARENT'S CARRY-ON CHECKLIST

☐ Plane gifts.

☐ Snacks. Try pre-cut fruit and protein bars—limit the sugary snacks. If there is an energy bar your kids will tolerate, bring a few. It's nice to be able to give your kids five grams of protein and the equivalent of a vitamin pill without a fuss. Remember to pre-cut the bar into a size that provides a reasonable dose of nutrition for your child.

☐ Empty water bottle. Fill it up at a water fountain after you clear security.

☐ Travel paperwork. Bring passports, copies of itinerary, hotel addresses, contact information, paper tickets, transportation reservations, and other key information. Note that just because it's on your phone, doesn't mean you will have easy access to the information at your new destination.

☐ A pull-up. Bring one even if your child has been using the potty for years. If the seatbelt sign is on, you can always do a quick change into the pull-up and keep the travel clothes dry. We carry ours in a resealable plastic bag doubling as camera padding!

☐ Valuables. Jewelry, electronics, wallet, and so on.

☐ Reading material. A book, magazine, or your e-Reader.

☐ Micro first-aid kit. See "First Aid Kit Ingredients" in chapter three.

If you are traveling with toddler(s) or infant(s):

☐ Change of clothes. Pack clothes in a resealable plastic bag. In the event of an accident the clean come out and the dirty go in.

☐ Bottle and formula. The bottle may need to start empty to clear security.

☐ Diapers.

☐ Wipes. Also very handy for in-air hand and face cleaning.

If you might get bumped, delayed, or are traveling to a destination with a high risk of lost luggage, carry on a "bump kit" in a resealable plastic bag with the air squeezed out at the bottom of your carry-on. Include:

☐ One clean shirt per person.

☐ One toothbrush per person.

☐ One pair of underwear per person.

☐ Essential (minimal) toiletries.

☐ Sleeping comfort essentials such as an extra bottle, pacifier, or favorite stuffed animal.

GETTING TO THE AIRPORT

Taxis are great once your kids have outgrown carseats. Before that, it's probably worth it to park at the airport or ask a friend to drive your family in your own car. If you won't need a carseat on your trip, you can just leave it buckled into your car. If you are bringing a carseat with you, you can remove it at the last minute. If you happen to have duplicate carseats and will be arriving back home exhausted or late at night, you might want to bring the extras with you on the trip. That way you don't have to fuss with reinstalling a seat when everyone is overtired and cranky after the return flight. Remember to have a plan for getting home. We don't recommend discount shuttle services as it's often cheaper to take one taxi than to buy seats for even two people in a discount shuttle; additionally, installing carseats securely is nearly impossible in most shuttle vans.

JUMPING THE HURDLES

Airports today present a series of gauntlets. The powers-that-be say to show up at the airport two hours ahead of your scheduled departure. Why not listen to reduce anxiety about missing the flight? Kid anticipation is usually at its peak when the day of departure arrives. Hopefully that excitement will carry them through the next couple of hours.

First, there's the airline check-in and baggage check process, which can be either straightforward, or a lengthy serpentine baggage-dragging experience. There's no need to drag the whole family through the line. You only need their passports and the bags for checking in. Kids and one parent can wait comfortably within view. Our kids, however, always seem to like the process of shuffling the bags a couple of feet and sitting down again on the big backpack. You can sometimes save time by checking in online before you arrive at the airport. Remember to always be kind to the check-in person! They have a tough job and they may also be able to do nice things for you and your family, from making sure that you are sitting together to upgrading you to a better class. It is also likely that this person will be the attendant at the gate, where they can include you in the bumping process or let that extra carry-on go unnoticed. Once bags are checked, you will be blissfully lighter on your feet.

Next comes airport security, which despite national and international standards still varies dramatically from place to place. The length of the line you may or may not have been in during check-in has no bearing on whether there will be a long wait at security. Try not to feel rushed. The kids will feel your stress, which will increase their anxiety level too. With uniformed security folks all around and the long line of fellow passengers behind you, the process will proceed much easier if everyone maintains their composure. Have your boarding passes and passports ready, move steadily, and most of all, do not make any security jokes (just kidding).

If you are traveling with a child in a stroller, you may be asked to go into a special line where security can deal with it more efficiently. Note that even sleeping children and infants in carseats must be disturbed, so don't count on naps lasting through security. Even if your baby has finally, finally, finally fallen asleep in his stroller, the TSA security officers still need you to take your baby out of the stroller, fold the stroller up, and stuff it through the x-ray machine. All alone, this is not easy! If you are alone, ask a stranger to help with the stroller. They'll be more than happy to help you keep the line moving. If you ask someone behind you, they'll be extra motivated. Other types of baby carriers must also go through x-rays, be prepared to remove your child and send the gear through..

GETTING "BUMPED"

Serendipitous travel is an art. A great opportunity to practice your serendipitous skills is getting bumped from an overbooked flight. When airlines sell too many tickets on a particular flight or flight changes and delays push too many passengers onto one flight, the airlines ask if anyone is willing to give up their seat in exchange for some compensation and a ticket for a later flight. This is called "getting bumped." Compensation packages vary from flight to flight and from airline

---

TRAVEL TIP: YOU JUST HAVE TO ASK!

Airline staff are generally happy to help you, especially when you have children. With most airlines, you can take your stroller or baby jogger up to the gate and leave it folded up at the end of the jetway. It will meet you right there when you arrive at your destination. Remember to ask the attendant at the gate for a tag if you want to use this service.

If you are having trouble negotiating the halls with all the kids and luggage, ask for a motorized assist and ride from gate to gate in one of those nifty chauffeur-driven, in-airport carts.

Traveling alone with kids? Remember that many of the other passengers are mothers, fathers, aunts, uncles, or grandparents. Just ask for a little help carrying something, finding something, or lifting something. Most folks will be happy to assist you. Of course, don't let your kids or your bags out of your sight or out of your control.

TIPS FOR GETTING "BUMPED"

- If you want to get "bumped," ask at the gate if the flight is oversold. Even if they do not think it will be oversold, ask the staff to start a list to be "bumped" and to put your name at the top. You never know what will happen and you'll start at the top of the list.
- Choose flights later in the day. Airline problems build up over the course of the day, increasing the likelihood of "bumping" on your flight.
- Don't avoid the crazy busy holidays. It can be painful to fly on Thanksgiving Sunday, but the increased odds of getting "bumped" can be a silver lining.
- Schedule a recovery day whenever you arrive somewhere. For example, if you have to be at an event on Monday, try to fly on Saturday. Then you can enjoy Sunday at your destination or you can take the "bump" without missing too much.
- Make sure to get all the details of how the airline will compensate you before agreeing to the "bump." Tell them that you will need a place to stay and meal vouchers.
- Get the details of when you will fly out before you give up your seats. Sometimes, a "bump" will actually get you to your destination earlier (or at nearly the identical time) because you get rerouted onto direct flights. It is dangerous to accept stand-by status on the next flight. Insist on a confirmed seat on a specific flight. You can also ask to stay overnight even if there is a later flight on the same day. In this case, you can enjoy the city, though the airline may be unwilling to pay for your lodging.
- Before accepting the "bump", check voucher expiration dates and limitations carefully to be sure you can use them.
- If you know that you want to fly to a small airport in the future that is serviced by the same airline, a round trip ticket voucher is the best deal as flights to small airports can be very expensive. If you are planning international travel in the near future, cash vouchers (for example, $300 off of the next flight) are a better deal because they can often be used on international flights. Read the fine print!
- And remember, always carry a "bump bag" in your carry-on, as described in this chapter's "The Parent's Carry-On Checklist."

to airline but they are often free round-tip tickets, vouchers toward future flights, or frequent flyer miles. If you have the time and flexibility, getting bumped can be an opportunity to see a new place (even if that place is only a hotel room for the night) and to get paid while you are at it (see "Tips for Getting Bumped"). To illustrate this point we present two real cases from our travel history:

- On a trip from Orlando to Seattle, we transferred through Memphis. In Memphis, we accepted a bump for three free round-trip tickets for our three seats (our youngest was still a lap baby). The airline also paid for a hotel and meals for twenty four hours. We rented the cheapest car we could find, saw the sights of Memphis (Graceland, the ducks at the Peabody Hotel, Beale Street, and the Lorraine Motel), and ate some delicious barbecued ribs (twice). Months later, we used the free tickets to visit family in Pennsylvania by flying into a small and usually expensive airport. On the way home from that trip, we got bumped again for $1,200 in travel vouchers. Although we spent that night in a dive hotel in Detroit questioning our own sanity, the following year we used the vouchers to offset the cost of a trip to visit friends in Japan. In the end, we got an impromptu and excellent tour of Memphis, a trip to see our family, and part of an international adventure.

- Before we even left our home airport in Seattle for a trip to Spain, we were offered a bump for $400 per ticket for our four seats. We declined at first because we were so excited to get out of town. Thankfully, we ran into an old friend about ten minutes later who screeched "What are you thinking?" We rushed back to the desk, volunteered our seats, and were given four vouchers that we exchanged for cash, in Euros, before departure. The airline put us up in a hotel (we did not want to go home again), fed us, and flew us out the next morning. Better connections got us to our destination only a few hours later than we were originally scheduled, and it was several weeks into the trip before we had to get more cash.

AWAITING DEPARTURE

You probably have some time to kill before the plane starts to board. Now is a good time to have a snack and make sure everyone is well hydrated. And do not forget to visit the bathroom before boarding. You will appreciate all the space in the airport bathrooms, especially if the younger members of your family need help in there. We have a traveling rule: when there is a chance to pee, everyone has to at least try. The rule enforcement begins at the airport.

If you still have time on your hands and energy to run off before the confinement of the plane, there are infinite creative ways to keep the kids active and

TWELVE ACTIVE ACTIVITIES FOR THE AIRPORT

1. Zogan's Game. Our kids love this game, and it can be as elaborate as your kids can handle given the space and the crowds. An adult gives instructions to the kids like "go around that pole twice, then do four jumping jacks, hop backward, go around the pole again, and then run to that line of trash cans. Jump up and down four times in front of the blue one then..." Following a list of eleven silly directions is actually pretty good brain training!

2. Travel Bingo (see sample card in chapter five).

3. Follow the Leader (don't be afraid to act silly in public).

4. Thumb-wrestling. Theoretically this is a quiet game but we can never keep it calm and quiet enough to play in a restaurant or on a plane.

5. Simon Says....

6. Yoga poses (you could bring a set of yoga flashcards).

7. A game of "school" in which you sit in your airport chairs and your child tells you what to do.

8. Browse the shop, come back, and tell me the silliest thing inside (no touching!).

9. People-to-People. Break into partners (two kids or one kid and one parent) and a parent calls out, for example, "ear-to-ear." The partners must move so that they are touching ear-to-ear. Start with the easy ones and ramp up. You can imagine the fun of "knee-to-ear" or "calf-to-chin."

10. How long can you balance on one foot? On one foot with your other foot on your knee (like a flamingo)? How long can you balance the cup on your head? On your elbow? How many hops can you make? How long can you walk on tiptoes? How high can you count?

11. Paper airplanes. Respect the space of others, of course, but there is usually enough empty space that kids can toss a plane and chase after it without disturbing anyone.

12. Counting game. How many black shirts can you see? Count the shoes in this waiting area. Are there more men or women? What fraction of the people on our plane do you think will be children? (Note that the kids should get up and walk around the waiting area of your gate to collect accurate information.)

engaged. Our family prefers active games that do not require any equipment, such as "Follow the Leader" (see "Twelve Active Activities for the Airport"). Our favorite game is one that we made up called "Zogan's Game" (a combination of our kids' names). Dodging the people in the terminal can be part of airport games, although don't let the kids get out of control and become a bother. Active games accomplish the duel purposes of using up time and tiring the kids out. Keep your kids within sight at all times. If quiet is more your style or you're hoping kids will sleep as soon as you board, try the activities for planes and restaurants described in "Fourteen Quiet Activities for the Plane" in this chapter and "Mealtime Is Family Time" in chapter five.

THE FLIGHT

Many airlines allow people traveling with small children to board early. This is great if you have lots of stuff or very small children, but since you packed so lightly, you may opt to reduce your on-plane time by ten minutes and board at the end of the line. Have your kids hand over the boarding passes and find the seats. Every engaged minute helps!

Once on board, just checking out their new surroundings—the stuff in the seatback pocket, and sometimes the pack of goodies on the seat (pillow, blanket, earphones, blindfolds, slippers, and so forth)—can entertain kids until the plane takes off. A few airlines are adept at entertaining kids on long flights and will have activity packets in children's hands before the plane even backs away from the gate. Activity packets may include coloring books, crayons, and even cheap video games. Unfortunately, you are not likely to see any of this stuff on budget airlines. Even on pricier airlines, kid giveaways and movies vary between flights, so none of it can be relied upon. On our last trans-Atlantic flight, even the in-flight movies failed! But here is where all your preparation is going to come in handy.

TRAVEL TIP: THE WONDERS OF A SIMPLE PLASTIC BAG

A simple trick makes deboarding a little easier and keeps your kids' belongings organized onboard: put all of your stuff in a plastic grocery bag before it goes into the seatback pocket. Nothing goes directly into the seatback pocket except trash waiting for a passing flight attendant. Everything you want to keep goes in and out of the bag. At the end of the flight, all the little toys, papers, books, homework assignments, and snacks are just pulled out of the pocket and popped back in the carry-on. (Give the seat pocket a final sweep just in case, especially the first few times you try this.)

Lay the Ground Rules

First of all, start by reminding your kids about their personal space and the rules for coexisting in cramped quarters. We have very strict rules about keeping feet off the seat in front of you (it's not your space) and not fiddling with the seatback tray table. Kids can use the table, but it doesn't go up-down, up-down, up-down. Think that's a silly rule? Just wait until you have a little kid sitting behind you! We also insist that everyone use the bathroom after meals and before landing (unless it is a very short flight). Having the whole family get up and down at the same time reduces chaos and reduces the chance for bathroom emergencies when the seatbelt sign is lit.

Keep Them Busy

While a long plane flight is a challenge, also think of it as forced quality time with your kids. Talk to them. Draw with them. Watch the movie with them or, if you can stomach it, try to watch their video game and be excited. With older kids, you can read the in-flight magazine together and talk about the articles. Share the content of your book and ask about theirs. Our young kids love to hear about cheap murder mysteries as we read (needless to say, we censor the content!). And they are even excited to hear about our science articles, figure out what a graph in the science paper displays, or consider the political slant of the nonfiction we are reading. How much time do you have in your normal life to hear about every exploit of Harry Potter in his fourth year at Hogwarts? Well, now is your chance to sit back and listen.

Movies are offered on most long flights. If there is one movie for the entire cabin, it's unlikely to be terribly kid-friendly. Sometimes personal video screens are on the back of every seat with a channel devoted entirely to kid shows and movies. If you are willing to subject your kids to mass Hollywood entertainment, the personal video screen can entertain your kids for hours. Our kids watched the same movie three or four times on one trans-Atlantic flight. Video screens also often feature an information channel displaying your plane as it moves along the route; watching this reminds the kids just where you're headed and how far you're traveling. If you've chosen

TRAVEL TIP: IN-FLIGHT PHOTOGRAPHY

Turn your cell phone to airplane mode (a mode in which it cannot send or receive a signal) before you shut it down at take-off. You can then turn it on during the flight to use as a camera. Silly in-flight photos and pictures taken out the window are great mementos and a fun way to pass the time.

FOURTEEN QUIET ACTIVITIES FOR THE PLANE

1. Try to guess how long one minute takes. For older kids, see if they can read for exactly ten minutes.

2. "I Spy with my little eye something that is…"

3. Drawing games: Start by drawing a circle or a blob and pass it to your child to finish. You can also pass the picture between all family members or take turns adding details until no one can think of anything else to add; pick a funny, made-up word and draw a picture to define it; try to tell a story over a series of pictures; share a picture by allowing each person to draw only one line at a time—if the pen gets picked up off the page, the turn is over; draw a picture with your eyes closed.

4. Tic-tac-toe. Add a challenge by making the grid bigger than the standard 3 by 3 square so the goal is to get four or, even six, in a row.

5. Hangman. You can pick a theme for words to make the game more engaging.

6. Dots. Create a matrix of dots; in each turn you add one line between two adjacent dots—up-and-down or across but not diagonally. If you close the box with its fourth line, put your initial inside and take another turn. The object of the game is to get the most boxes.

7. Crossword puzzles, word searches, and unscramble games. For younger children, make your own.

8. Create a maze and have your child solve it. Have your child create a maze for you to solve.

9. Math and word puzzle books. Books of optical illusions are also really fun; then try to create your own.

10. String games such as Cat's Cradle and Jacob's Ladder. Finger knitting and crocheting are also quiet and engaging.

11. Fortune tellers. Have each person write his or her name on the top of a blank piece of paper and fold it over once. Mix up the papers and pass them out again. Have each person write down the name of a city and fold it over. Mix the papers up again. Write down a number from one to ten, fold, and mix. Write down an adjective, fold, and mix. Eventually, you unfold each paper and read out the fortune: "<Billy> will live in <London> and have <seven> children. His wife will be <crazy> and they will <hop> a lot."

12. Make up a Mad Lib for your family as you wait for the meal to be delivered and then fill it in after the meal when you have all forgotten the details.

13. Crazy animal. Fold a blank paper in half and make two small pencil marks on the fold. The pencil marks should be visible from both sides. Have one child secretly draw a fanciful head on one side, using the pencil marks to define the neck. Pass the paper to another child without letting them see the head and have them draw a body on the back side, also using the pencil marks as a neck. Open the picture!

14. Toothpicks. Lay down three rows of toothpicks (pencils, straws, sugar packs also work) as follows:

In each turn, a person can take as many toothpicks as they want from a single row. The object of the game is not to take the last toothpick.

to bring a laptop or DVD player, you can completely control the content and timing of this easy entertainment.

What else can you do? Kids can explore the contents of their carefully-packed carry-ons. The box "Fourteen Quiet Activities for the Plane" provides additional suggestions for entertainment. Activities are aimed at a variety of ages and, with a little creativity, can be modified to meet the needs of a young child or a clever teenager.

Bring Out the Gifts

When you've run out of easy conversation and digital entertainment is either not available, not allowed, or too boring, it's time for those in-flight surprises. Hopefully, they will also help you pass some enjoyable time together. A new coloring book, for example, is way more fun when enjoyed with parents. Plus, when you share the experience with them, they are more likely to color attentively or wrestle with a puzzler for more than one minute before begging for another mini-gift. As we mentioned earlier, mete these gifts out slowly to make them last.

Look Out the Window

Pictures of Earth from space are always impressive. We gain perspective, learn geology, see our own hometown in a new way, and maybe even pick up a little geography. On a plane flight, why not spend some time looking out the window with your kids?

Look out the window as you take off. Try to spot some key landmarks to help your kids orient themselves from the air. It's one thing to know that there is a lake near downtown but another to actually see it. Point out the highways, rivers, and special attractions. Bring a copy of *Windowseat: Reading the Landscape from the Air,* by Gregory Dicum. It's a great introduction to the things you can explore from the air with special sections for each region of the U.S. The book

IN-FLIGHT BREASTFEEDING

Flying with a baby might seem intimidating, but it is much easier than flying with a toddler, so enjoy it while it lasts. Infants don't cry particularly loudly, they don't want to get up and run around, they don't kick the seat in front of them, grab germy handrails, order sugary drinks, play loud video games, or loudly say embarrassing things about other people. In exchange for a little milk, they typically will lie peacefully through the whole ordeal.

Breastfeeding can be a little stressful when you are also in shoulder-to-shoulder contact with a stranger. On Ashley's first flight alone with baby, she was seated next to a young guy in a fancy business suit. There was no way to be discrete and the moment seemed extremely awkward. The man smiled, and said, "Oh, I remember the first in-flight feedings. They were tough." That thoughtful comment transformed the planeful of serious men into a cabin of dads-who-miss-their-kids-and-totally-understand-what-it-might-be-like-to-be-flying-alone-with-a baby. Your flights will also be full of dads, uncles, and granddads, not to mention other mothers!

On business trips without baby, you may have to get your pump and breastmilk through security. This is really not a big deal. TSA security officers have seen breastpumps before, honest. And mothers are currently allowed to bring breastmilk through security (more than three ounces) as long as they declare the milk to the security officer. Currently, even moms traveling without their babies can take breastmilk through security. Breastmilk is in the same category as liquid medications. You should keep it separate from your other liquids and present it for inspection. You won't be asked to taste it (phew!), but you may be asked to open the container, and it might be tested for explosives. When traveling with a baby or toddler, you may also bring formula or juice through security in quantities over three ounces but, again, you need to declare it and present it for inspection. Up-to-date details are available at the TSA website (tsa.gov/travelers/airtravel/children/formula.shtm).

also includes just the right amount of detail about how to look for and understand glaciation and plate tectonics.

What you see out the window will depend on both where you are and when you're there. If it's a cloudy day, there's not much you can do about that. On clear days, however, you can see the world from your seat. You've already prepared your kids for your trip by looking at a map. You may have selected a few things you'd really like to look for on your flight: a mountain, a military base, a desert, or a city. Now's the time to really see evidence of plate tectonics, glaciation, watersheds, and other features you researched when getting ready. The more your children learned about the large forces that shape what you see from the air, the more excited they will be when they see them on the ground. Window fun can continue when the sun goes down. During night flights, take a look at how many lights you can see. How are they distributed? Why are some areas particularly lit up? Where are the darkest areas and why?

Why not make a scavenger hunt from the window? Things to include might be: lake, car, truck, road, factory, open pit mine, river, dam, airport, school, windmill, red house, blue house, power lines, forest, fire, city, highway, round irrigated field, square agricultural field, and so on. Younger kids can simply search for geometric shapes and colors; older kids can hunt for complex detail. Your kids could also create a scavenger hunt list on your outbound flight based on what they spot out the window to use on the way home.

ARRIVING

Although your plane has landed and you are about to disembark into a new and exciting world, you are not quite free of plane travel logistics. Everyone is probably tired if it was a long flight. Combine exhaustion with the excitement of arrival and the immediate business of immigration, baggage claim, customs, and finding transport to your lodging, and there is high potential for chaos. There is a funny and telling YouTube video of Bjork arriving at the Bangkok airport after a long flight and inexplicably wrestling with a reporter who had the nerve to ask her a question. You do not want your flight weariness to get the better of you, even if the press is not outside your gate.

Prepare your kids for arrival, particularly in the case of international travel. Immigration cards need to be filled out, sometimes one for every member of the family, and you need to account for all your bags. Remind the kids (and yourself) that this is an important part of traveling, and that there are not a lot of things more exciting than coming through the customs doors into the airport lobby of an alien city and finding your way. Explain the steps of arrival in advance. First, immigration officers look at your documents and let you into the country. Then, you grab your checked luggage and head to customs. Customs officers look at your stuff and your documents and then they permit you to bring your stuff into the country. Many kids have some anxiety about being inspected by uniformed (or possibly armed) officials, so give the process a positive spin: these people are keeping everyone safe. There is no reason to rush these sometimes complicated and confusing steps. Take the arrival process as it comes and don't feel any pressure to move quickly and get out fast. Play a few games or review phrases in the local language if lines are long.

You may need to find a currency exchange or an ATM once you're through customs. Be particularly alert changing or getting money at the airport since it's an obvious place for dishonest folks to target travelers. Wait to get cash until you are in a secure and well-lit location. Keep large bills separate from small bills to avoid displaying lots of cash in the taxi or when buying a bus ticket.

You probably booked at least your first night's lodging in advance. You may have even done a little background research on ground transportation options for getting you and your family from the airport to the hotel. Taxis from airports might have been an expensive option when you were a single person backpacking through a developing country, but as a family, a taxi is often the cheapest and easiest option; its efficiency may even be worth a splurge if your group is nearing the edge of exhaustion. If you still have energy, the bus, train, or subway can provide an economical and environmentally-friendly introduction to a city. More and more cities offer efficient public transportation between the airport and the downtown core. Regardless, you can finally put some of those phrases you've been memorizing to use!

When you check into your hotel, ask to see the room first as there may be options. Know that, in many countries, the hotel desk may ask to keep your passport. This is normal, but remember to get your passport back before you leave. As you sit on the bed in your new room, enjoy. You're officially finished jumping the hurdles, awaiting departure, sitting still in a plane, and arriving at an unfamiliar airport. You are ready to enjoy a new location and all it has to offer.

THE PLANE TRUTH

All in all, the airplane portion of your trip can be fraught with details and logistics. With patience, planning, and fortitude, it can also be a wonderful part of your adventure. You have time with your kids to talk, play, cuddle, and enjoy. If you approach the journey with an open mind and a can-do attitude, the fun can begin at lift-off when you are officially "on the loose."

5 Living on the Loose

Now that your plane has touched down and you're settled into your first night's lodging, the real trip begins! This will not be a second honeymoon, an extreme adventure, or a respite from reality. You will be traveling, night and day, with your children. Patience you once applied to companions who got sick on long bus rides or spent too much time calculating tips at restaurants will now be tested with your new companions and their unique traveling quirks. Pack yourself an extra paperback and surrender to siestas if you think they might get tired in the afternoons. Add a castle to your itinerary if they live for princesses. In this chapter, we provide fun suggestions for everyday logistics, from taking turns when making decisions to finding food that you will all love eating.

PLANNING YOUR DAY

Unless you booked a full-service package tour, multiple choices will be made on the road every day. These decisions may be large (where are we going today?) or small (which postcard should we buy?). Involve your kids as much as possible in deciding what to do each day. Nobody wants to feel that they are being dragged around the globe without any control or chance to contribute. Even a two-year-old can answer questions like, "Should we sit inside or outside?" and, "Do you want to walk through the park or down the street?" When kids help shape the direction of the day, they have ownership of the trip. Everyone shares expectations about activities, snacks, souvenirs, walking distances, and meals.

Dealing with Jetlag

As you plan your first days on the loose, try to use time changes and odd sleep-

The dollar store concept apparently has international appeal. We've found 100 Yen shops in Japan and one Euro shops across Europe. They're everywhere. It's all plastic junk, but it's cheap. The souvenir budget can go a long way in a "dollar" store and browsing the aisles can even offer a glimpse into another culture. Your kids will naturally compare the inexpensive trinkets in other countries and their own. They might also find some entertainment for restaurants and bus rides. These shops aren't usually in the higher-rent tourist areas, so you may need to ask a local. Visiting a different part of town is all part of the fun.

ing schedules to your advantage. See things during the hours that you feel wide awake and ready to go. Unique opportunities appear at the margins of the normal day. If you are heading east of your home turf and naturally staying up later in the evening, take advantage of your sleep schedule by dining late, admiring the city lights, or going to an evening show your kids would normally miss. Restaurants in places like Spain do not even open until eight or nine in the evening, and European streets at night have an excited vibe that sleeps during the day. Your kids will be able to witness this energy soon after you arrive when they can't sleep anyway. If you travel west, waking up earlier than usual, take advantage by watching the sunrise, seeing the city awaken, or visiting the early morning market. The Tsukiji fish market in Tokyo, for example, is most exciting before dawn when most Japanese are still asleep. The sight of Thai monks collecting alms at sunrise is another opportunity for the jetlagged.

Eventually everyone's sleep schedule will evolve to approximate the local time, but you do not need to be in a hurry. Depending on how far you've traveled, it could take a few days or a week. A helpful rule of thumb is that it takes about one day per hour of time change to adjust. Avoid making commitments at the wrong end of the day at the beginning of your trip, before you've been able to acclimatize. Exploring the morning market in Marrakech, meeting work friends for a formal dinner, or witnessing the full moon of May in Bodh Gaya might be easier for everyone to handle once you're on local time.

As you adapt to local time, try to maintain the same sleep schedule as your kids so that you get some rest too. Staying awake to get onto local time while your kids will be waking up on home time does not lead to a pleasant day. If you always go to bed about an hour after your kids, keep that pattern up on the road. Don't try to push yourself out of jetlag by staying up four hours after your kids pass out, even if that would put you on the correct local time. Kids are going to wake up when they wake up and you definitely want to be rested when that happens.

If you absolutely need to get onto local time quickly, remember that it is a lot easier to make kids stay awake than it is to make them go to sleep. Even for adults, falling asleep when our circadian clock says to be awake is simply impossible and lying awake in a hotel room can be a miserable experience. If you need to get onto local time quickly, wake yourself on local time even if it means waking up on only a few hours of sleep. Force yourself (and your family) to stay awake until local bedtime. If by chance, you end up wide awake in a hotel room at 4 a.m., make the best of it! One of Ashley's fondest memories of traveling as a child is a 2 a.m. picnic in a hotel room, looking out over the lights of London.

What to do?

One simple idea for keeping your kids engaged is to take turns planning the day. A professor we know traveled around Europe in a camper van with his two teenage children; every fourth day, the whole family did whatever one member chose and planned. He reminisces about one kid who always chose the local zoo or something to do with natural history, while the other always planned a physical outdoor adventure. When it was the adults' turn to design the day, mom or dad opted for something totally different—a museum, city tour, or quiet day at

BASICS OF CULTURAL RESPECT

In preparing your kids, it is essential to discuss the issue of cultural respect. You and your family will be representing your home country as you travel. The following list is a good place to start:

- Don't point your finger or your camera directly at anyone, and ask before taking pictures.
- Speak quietly.
- Keep your feet off public property such as benches, train seats, and statues.
- Dress modestly in modest cultures and in religious centers.
- Line up politely in countries where others do the same. Don't get bent out of shape about mob-lines in countries where this is standard operating procedures. (Don't worry, you'll know which is which very quickly!)
- Say "thank you."
- Don't stare.
- Begin with "Excuse me. Do you speak English?" in the native language if you can.
- Review in advance any unique aspects of cultural etiquette for each destination.

the beach. Of course, if you don't want your children wielding quite that much power, take turns making smaller daily choices, such as choosing the restaurant or what time the family wakes up in the morning.

Another way to plan your day is to give it a theme. You might plan a day around a book, (*Madeline in Paris*), or around an epoch (medieval life). Visiting a museum or a historical monument is more fun with context. Sometimes we also try out themes like "Tourist Day," in which we really pack in the obvious tourist attractions, or "Real Life Day," in which we live like locals. Taking a day off from traditional tourism for "every day" adventures can give you and your kids more opportunities for interaction with locals and a closer glimpse of daily life. Visit a small park in your hotel's neighborhood where local kids are playing, splash in a fountain on a hot day, visit a market to buy fresh fruit or a bakery to buy pastries, or browse a "dollar" store (see "Cheap Souvenir Tip: International "Dollar" Stores"). "Real Life Day" is also the perfect opportunity to get a haircut and wash your clothes! (See the section "Explore the Local Life" in chapter six for more ideas.)

Avoiding the Urge to Overschedule

Our guiding philosophy for scheduling is to make the most of every day! A great schedule includes time to explore and opportunities for spontaneity. Resist packing each day with wall-to-wall activities. If you can remember back, it wasn't much fun constantly racing from one site to another when you traveled before kids. Now you have an excuse to put fun first: it's for the kids! Expanding an activity to fill unexpected free time is always possible, but trying to squeeze in too many activities is likely to create friction and exhaustion. Will you have a better day rushing to three big destinations or would you all have more fun enjoying just two of the spots and spending the extra time eating pastries and feeding the ducks? You won't get to see every painting in Paris or every artifact in Egypt, but you can certainly hit the highlights while enjoying a fun and adventurous learning experience.

Unscheduled time is often the most magical. You finished the temple tour and you're not yet hungry for dinner? That's when you find a cool path that leads behind the temple to an enchanting garden. Browsing slowly to kill time? You're a lot more likely to start chatting with the shopkeeper and get invited to tea. Once, with a sore foot that kept us from completing our day's hike on the Cotswold Way in England, we browsed and chatted so long in a little shop that we ended up spending the night in a spare room upstairs! What you don't plan is likely to be the best part of the trip.

PARENTING ON THE ROAD

Your kids are your traveling companions. They are fun and insightful. They have participated in planning the trip, they are helping to make decisions about what to do each day, and they are even showing you new opportunities for cultural exchange. However, they are the children and you are still the parents.

Keeping Your Kids Prepared

Knowing what's going to happen next helps all of us feel confident and relaxed. This is especially true for children. Kids thrive when they know what is expected of them and what is on the schedule. Home routines like wake up, dress, eat breakfast, brush teeth, and grab the backpack on the way out provide structure and comfort for kids. They need to be reminded about the details, but they can engage and contribute more fully when they have the big picture and don't encounter too many unexpected tasks.

This need-to-know is even more pronounced when traveling. If kids know what is on their schedule for the next five minutes, five hours, and five days, they can be active participants rather than excess baggage. If you drag your kids off to dinner just when they thought they could flop on the hotel bed and surf all those new TV channels, they're not going to be thrilled. Or if you announce that this is the last day in Hat Yai, just when your son figured out how to walk from the hotel to the *kanom* shop by himself, he's going to be frustrated. Keep your kids informed because they're happier when they know what's coming around the bend.

Managing Ebbs and Flows

There will be natural highs and lows on the road. They may be similar to those you experience at home, but they may be magnified on a trip. These ebbs and flows might have a daily, weekly, or even monthly rhythm. On a daily scale, there may be a predictable sleepy period in the afternoon, even if your kids have long ago given up napping. It's often easier not to fight this natural low. Instead, take advantage of the lull by building afternoon relaxation into the daily schedule— reading a book in your hotel room, resting in a café, or sitting by a pond—until everyone's batteries are recharged. And of course there is also that all-time, perfect rejuvenator: afternoon ice cream!

On the other end of the energy spectrum, kids tend to get bursts of giggly energy late in the day when they are tired. At home this frequently happens right at bedtime. Frustratingly, it often happened to us earlier when traveling and we ended up struggling at restaurants. Since it's hard to channel this energy into anything constructive, it's generally easier to enjoy the burst than to control it. Schedule some time for running around a park, battling a controlled pillow fight, or singing at a deserted bus stop. Experiment with the timing of your energy-burning diversions in order to take advantage of their quiet energy right at dinner or bedtime, when you need it most.

On longer time scales, homesickness may also come and go. Homesickness affects each child differently but it is often cyclical. Expect a bit of gloominess a couple of days or a couple of weeks into the trip. The comfort of a familiar, messy room piled with stuffed animals, sports mementos, and photos is easy to underestimate. Younger kids can have a tough time understanding that they will return home after the trip. Older kids will likely miss friends, worry that they're being left out, and chafe at the lack of certain kinds of independence that they enjoy at home. Homesickness can set in quickly, even when you are having fun; it's a natural part of being away from home. Homesick feelings don't need to be swept under the carpet. They can be acknowledged by writing postcards to family, buying small presents for friends, or sharing a familiar activity that you often enjoy at home. You could also try eating American food, playing a favorite game, or watching an American movie. Journaling can be a helpful, private outlet for your kids (see chapter seven, "The World's Best Travel Journal").

Turning Bad Behavior Around

All kids, whether on the road or at home, misbehave at times. One of the challenges of traveling is that discipline methods you employed successfully at home may no longer work. You can't send your kids to their rooms, make them clean the kitchen, or ground them. Additionally, all the routines that help you maintain good behavior will be thrown to the wind. Discipline techniques and comforting routines may need to be completely reinvented. In order to set your kids up for success on the road, start by developing strategies that encourage good behavior in your kids: afternoon quiet time, breakfast in the room, or teenagers-on-their-own time. Consistent pre-bedtime journal writing or morning postcards in the café can prevent arguments about when is a good time to settle down and do some thinking or writing. Also, be mindful of the natural three-meals-a-day eating cycle. Eating a serious lunch while you're out and about may be expensive or inconvenient, but it's emotionally cheaper and significantly easier than hunger meltdowns.

Traveling is a good time to loosen some limits and allow a later bedtime one night, an extra afternoon sugary treat, or a mini-shopping spree for souvenirs. But be forewarned: although parents know that the old limits are simply widened temporarily, kids might assume that the limits are gone altogether. Kids can become bratty, angry, or confused when they smack against the new limits. Figuring out how to set and navigate the travel limits is good learning for everyone involved, but this learning can be painful. As always, setting clear expectations can help minimize the transition. When you broaden the rules, be explicit. "Let's go get a souvenir. You can buy one thing and it has to cost less than ten Euros. If you haven't found anything in twenty minutes, then the deal's off and we can try again later on the trip."

No matter how fantastic your parenting skills and preparation, eventually you will have to deal with bad behavior. Likely it will be in public, you will be exhausted, and you will not be able to find an easy immediate consequence for even the worst behavior. First, be prepared to abandon your immediate plans— you may have to skip the sit-down restaurant or last museum trip. Next, make sure that you don't try to placate misbehaving kids with McDonald's, a playground, or an ice cream. Treats just reward your kids for a tired temper fit. You need to have a plan in advance for checking the misbehavior. Here are a few suggestions for on-the-go discipline for all ages:

- In the morning, you can tell them that you will withhold the afternoon treat if their behavior doesn't meet your expectations. You either have to follow through and deny the treat while the rest of the family enjoys it or allow them to earn it back through better behavior.
- Time outs are still a possibility but they require more work from you. You clearly can't leave your kids on a chair in the corner of a museum or alone sitting on a bench when they get a time out, you must take a time out too. You, however, can enjoy it. Pull a paperback out of your bag, take the chance to review the city map, or finish up a postcard. Of course, don't let your kid do anything constructive or fun while you enjoy your mini-break.
- Invest in an incentive system. Pick something cheap and fun like beads or coins. Whenever they do a great job, they get one. When things go poorly, they lose one. When they accumulate ten, they get a privilege like picking the next restaurant, a souvenir, or getting their bag carried for a whole day. You will need an easy supply of your incentive items and they will need a way to store them. Something with a hole that can slide on a keychain works nicely and something relevant is always neat: locally-made African beads, Chinese coins with square holes, old European coins with holes in the middle, Indian bangles, or Guatemalan colored bracelets.
- You can record their behavior in their journal. Better not to write where they write as this is crossing a privacy boundary. In the back of the journal, you can

rate the day and then offer a reward for three days in a row above a pre-set threshold. This system works best for older kids who don't need immediate consequences.

- Teachers know discipline, so borrow some tried and true classroom strategies. Classrooms across the country get a reward such as a party for filling up a jar with marbles. Similarly, you could put stickers on a card full of squares. Alternately, many classrooms are managed by the distribution of green, red, or yellow cards or sticks—green for great behavior, yellow for on-the-edge, and red for bad. Distribute these as necessary, using perhaps colored bracelets or beads instead. If your child still has a red card or stick at the end of the day, he gets a punishment. The consequence (the red or yellow item) is immediate and can be doled out in public, but the punishment, such as an early bedtime or a withheld toy, can be managed later in the privacy of the hotel room.

PLAYING IT SAFE

As parents you are no doubt already experienced and obsessed with keeping your children safe. Safety expectations and standards are culturally driven, however,

FINDING A SITTER

We generally don't use sitters while traveling but it can sometimes be refreshing for you and your kids to have a night away from each other. The first rule is safety. Don't take any chances. In developing areas, we don't recommend leaving your kids with anyone except longtime friends. Remember, if $10 US is a month of wages, devious folks will be willing to invest a great deal of time in developing a friendship that could eventually lead to cash, blackmail, passports, theft of electronics, or worse. That's not to say that most people aren't wonderful. They are. Enjoy them. Invest in friendships. Just don't leave your kids with the wonderful woman who has been so helpful for weeks but who you met at the train station.

In developed countries and urban centers, you can apply the same strategies you would at home. Start with references from friends. Even references from friends of friends are better than the internet. Big hotels and resorts often have babysitting services. If you expect that you will want a date night or know that you have an invitation to the ball, you might plan a night or two at a particularly reputable hotel or resort so that you can take advantage of their sitting services. If you plan to use a sitting service or a friend of a friend, check references in advance by phone, Skype, or e-mail.

and they may vary widely from country to country. Laws, rules, and cultural norms can be vastly different from the American expectation that everything will be made safe for you (or else you can speak to my lawyer). A little advance research on topics that pertain to staying safe in particular countries can be very important.

We're Not in Kansas Anymore

In most countries, personal safety is the responsibility of each person. Dangers aren't necessarily carefully identified and labeled; construction areas aren't necessarily cordoned off with miles of yellow flagging. The Australian joke is that Americans have signs in the forest that read "Watch Out for Falling Branches!" and more signs up saying "Please Read Safety Signs to Prevent Injury." And before you even get a chance to go into the forest, you have to sign a waiver promising that if you don't read the signs and you do get hit by a falling branch, you won't sue. The U.S. legal system instills a belief that we are entitled to safety and if an accident occurs, we can hold someone else responsible. We have warnings about hot coffee, legal limits to the temperature of tap water, and mandatory smoke alarms. This is not a worldwide phenomenon.

Individual responsibility is generally the norm. Balcony railings aren't necessarily sturdy enough to lean on and there is no one checking ahead that the spaces between the railings of the balcony are narrow enough to prevent your toddler from falling through. Uneven sidewalks may sound minor but they require more energy and concentration for walking safely. And watch out for that shin-high pipe sticking out of the wall. Instead of counting on everyone else to ensure a safe ledge, window, water tap, or road crossing, you need to survey an area yourself and ensure the safety of you and your children. This doesn't mean that there is danger leaping out at you from around every corner; it just means that you should check around the corner to assess the situation for yourself.

Look Both Ways

The first task on the kid safety agenda is to teach your kids about safety in the street. Though you will always try, you can't always be right there to protect them from everything. Your kids will need some focused education about the risks of walking down the street in a strange new place. Try to balance your natural parental paranoia about safety with confidence and practicality; you don't want to terrify them. But most kids don't have much experience crossing chaotic intersections, hopping on and off buses, running for trains, or waving down taxis. Many places don't have sidewalks, and bikes or even motorcycles may weave in and out of pedestrians where there are sidewalks. Your kids will be distracted and tired; stay diligent, especially in a place where cars drive on the other side of the road and you're not used to looking for them in that direction. This has become such an issue in high tourist areas of London that they've painted signs on the road at street crossings saying which way to look. In places like Amsterdam, it's not only the cars you have to watch out for when crossing the street; bicycles and trams have their own designated lanes alongside.

Don't Talk to Strangers

This can be more difficult on the road than at home. Parameters of cultural etiquette vary widely. In many cultures it is perfectly okay, and even expected, that strangers approach and speak to children. Storekeepers might offer candy; temple or museum staff might invite your kids to see something special. Foremost, keep your kids safe, but try not to interfere with the many innocent and wonderful culture exchanges that make travel rewarding.

Come up with some guidelines in advance. For example, kids may take candy or food when offered, say thank you (in the native language), and smile. But they must wait for your okay to eat it. You can have a sign, like a little nod, if it's okay for them to indulge. Without the nod, they simply carry the food until you can check it out and make a decision. Kids shouldn't go out of your range of vision with a stranger—ever. They can follow, but they must invite you along too. And traveling is a great opportunity to learn to spot a drunk reaching out to the naïve or to identify likely pick-pocket scenarios. Talk to your kids about what you see, when you see it. "See that guy, he's suspiciously getting too close," or, "I think this could be a scam because ...," or "I didn't trust her." Build street sense.

United We Stand, Divided We Call

Many of the places you go will be packed with other people. Holding hands works pretty well as a tool to stay close to your kids in crowds, but you can't hold their hands all day long. You should establish a plan for what to do if you get separated. Quiz your kids on the plan frequently so that they won't forget it in the event it's needed. Your plan should include dynamic situations, like when someone boards a tram but the others are still talking on the platform (everyone meet at the next stop). Consider buying disposable prepaid cell phones so that reuniting is only a programmed telephone call away. This may not be financially practical for short trips or in places with spotty cell phone coverage, but we ended up relying on our eight-year-old's phone more often than we thought we would. For kids too young to handle the responsibility of a phone, you can get bracelets engraved with local and long-distance emergency telephone numbers, just in case. They make a nice travel souvenir, too (see "Travel Tip: Emergency Bracelets and Allergy Alerts," in chapter one).

Wash Your Hands

Of course, washing your hands is always a good idea before you eat, but it is also smart after you've been in a museum with hundreds or thousands of other people from all over the world, holding the same banisters and turning the same doorknobs. While traveling, your kids will be exposed to new ideas and new cultures, and they'll also be exposed to new bacteria and new viruses. There's no need to panic by wearing masks and rubber gloves; just get in the habit of using

TRAVEL TIP: EVERYONE LIKES A MAP

Here's a great keepsake for your kids! It's cheap, fun, educational, and functional. Find a decent tourist map of whatever city you happen to be visiting and give your son or daughter a highlighter and a pen. Along the way, highlight your route, marking and annotating where you are and what you are seeing. Want to make a really cool map? You'll have to be willing to walk a long way! Keep the maps from various places as a reminder of where you traveled, what you saw, and what your kids enjoyed most.

hand sanitizer periodically and try to keep your kids from stuffing their fingers in their mouths. Kids are, by definition, kids. So have patience and a sense of humor. We have a friend who held both of her son's hands at fast food restaurants to prevent germs. One day she glanced down to see her son running his tongue directly along the counter. Yum!

GETTING AROUND

You usually have multiple options for getting around while traveling, from jumping on a subway to hiring a car to using your own two feet. One day you'll use one method. The next day, you may try something totally different. The best choice depends on many factors including availability, cost, energy, daily goals, and the needs of your family.

Walking

A big part of any trip is walking. Whether it's strolling through a museum, hiking across the mountains, or walking out to the pool, your kids will be on their feet. As you know, the younger the child, the shorter the distance they can walk without getting tired—they have to take more steps with those short legs. You can

CITY SCAVENGER HUNT

Planning a big day or two of tourist activities? Make a scavenger hunt for your kids. Copy internet photos of famous icons for younger kids and offer checkboxes when they finally see it. Provide big empty spaces on the page and ask your kids to draw other famous landmarks. Ask questions of older kids that they'll need to work to answer. For example, "What year was the Seattle Space Needle built?" or, "How many ships are in the harbor and what sort of ships are they?" Older kids can even make a scavenger hunt for you and, accidentally, they'll end up researching your destination and finding local hot spots to visit. If your kids can handle a little friendly competition, assign points and see who can collect the most over the day. We provide a sample city scavenger hunt at the end of this chapter that you can photocopy to use anywhere or modify for a specific destination.

cope with walking in lots of ways. First, it'll help the kids' perspective on the day if they know how much walking they will be expected to do before you set out. If the plan is for everyone to walk to the temple before lunch, then they know when the walking will end and you can help motivate them along the way. Conversely, if they learn that when they whine you will carry them, they're more likely to get tired quickly.

Build "walking pride." Log kid miles (or kilometers—they can get in a little math doing the conversion and the numbers build faster), and encourage them to time themselves. Map your route on Google Earth or track your distance with your smart phone. Start slowly with the walking. Walking five miles on day one might bring about a revolt and a taxi on day two. Walking one mile on day one and being challenged to walk two miles on day two could lead to an ice cream cone and a willingness to walk three miles on day three. Try tricks: race one block (speed walking, no running); tiptoe until you get to the shade; count your steps for one block. Compare the number of steps per block going north to south with the number of steps per block going east to west. Walk until you pass the first store with a letter "G" in the name or until you pass the first big tree. Walk until you find the whole alphabet on signs—in order. Guess how many steps it will take to get to the gallery and then offer a two-minute piggy back ride to the kid who guesses closest without going over. And, finally, encourage everyone to wear good shoes. For the love of popsicles, don't wear flip-flops.

Of course the littlest kids will eventually need a stroller or a backpack ride if serious walking is part of your plan. Plan ahead. Light strollers are easy to bring along but take a pounding on uneven sidewalks and can rarely navigate nature trails. More rugged strollers are easier to maneuver on bumpy surfaces but are heavier and bulkier, making them harder to transport. The last time we traveled with a stroller, we opted for a cheap and light folding version, expecting it to fall apart through the course of the trip and not expecting to bring it home again. Sure enough, by the last week it was held together with bits of bent coat hangers from a hotel closet. But we did get three hard weeks out of it on the cobblestones of Italy.

Public Transportation

In most cities of the world, public transportation—subways, buses, trains, trams, ferries, funiculars, and gondolas—is a fun and economical choice. In Europe or Japan, for instance, there is no need to even consider renting a car if you are staying in a city. Public transportation is so well developed in these places that it accesses almost every neighborhood. As a well-used public resource, these transportation systems are usually safe for you and your kids, with the exception of rougher neighborhoods, late nights, or particularly busy times. Have you seen the video of white-gloved attendants pushing riders into the trains during Tokyo rush hour? Many of us wouldn't feel comfortable in that situation even without kids.

Public transportation ticket plans and payment schemes can be confusing and they differ widely from place to place. Most transportation systems have two payment schemes—one for tourists and another for the local community. Some payment schemes demand separate payments or tickets every time you step on a bus or subway, while others offer multiday passes for all types of transportation in the region. If you stay long enough, you might be able to save money with a monthly pass. Explore options and choose the best for your family and for your length of stay.

In most places, children under a certain age are free or pay reduced fares. Purchasing these reduced fare tickets may require a little extra time waiting in line at the window instead of using the automated machine. Also be aware of the many ways of paying for a ride. In some cities, you pay up front before you enter a train; in others, you pay a conductor while you are on the train. Lots of transportation systems now use honor systems; you don't submit your ticket and plain-clothed transit police randomly sweep though trains to ensure that all riders have valid tickets, fining those without.

In tourist destinations, access to public transportation may be included on "city cards" for a fixed amount of time. These cards, purchased from hotels or other tourist centers, are usually valid for 24, 48, or 72 hours and allow access to museums, tours, and other attractions for free or for reduced rates. If you are planning on seeing the attractions anyway, the cards can provide a significant savings.

Relying on public transportation outside of major cities is more complicated. While in some countries it is easy, in others it can be challenging or unavailable. In Austria, train lines serpentine through almost every valley, linking transportation hubs in the cities with small rural villages. In turn, these villages give access via foot, funicular, and tram to alpine hut-to-hut hiking. In Central America, we found buses that accessed nearly every village but the more remote destinations had less frequent service and bare-bones buses. American suburbs and small towns can be truly impossible to navigate by public transportation alone.

Travel Bingo!

Need something to do while you're walking or waiting for the bus? Try travel bingo! Copy ours or have your kids make their own to suit your location. Ask the hotel desk to make a few photocopies so the whole family can play. Make sure you have a pencil or two for everyone to mark their finds as they see them.

B	I	N	G	O
Woman in uniform	College sweatshirt	Kid with backpack	Man in colorful shirt	Boy in baseball hat
Teenager with piercing	Baby in stroller	Man with gray hair	Soldier	Woman in black dress
Man on a bicycle	Obviously dyed hair	FREE	Grandma with grand-kids	Crying baby
People holding hands	Three women talking	Dog not on a leash	An ugly shirt	Man with tattoo
Girl in boots	Man with beard	Teenager wearing headphones	Pregnant woman	Ripped jeans

Private Transportation

Private cabs, rickshaws, tuk-tuks, and bike rentals are all fun options and often add local color to the journey. Taxicabs in London, for example, have little seats that fold down for riding backward. They aren't comfortable but kids love them. If there are enough people in your party, taxis can be a reasonably economical option. Of course, if you are late for an engagement, carrying weary children, or have blistered feet, taxis are worth paying a premium. Beware of taxis that do not charge using a meter. If there is no meter, barter for the fare in advance. Do your homework and know about how much the fare should be. Beware of cabs offering overpriced tourist rates for short rides.

Kids and traffic don't mix well. Some auto taxi drivers do carry kid seats or boosters in their trunk, so ask if they are available. If you phone for the cab, request a car with child seats. At the very least, make sure kids are strapped in appropriately with seat belts where available. Consider safety when you explore other forms of private transportation. Motorcycle taxis are off limits for our family.

Big cities often host private "hop-on, hop-off" tourist buses on routes that cover all the major attractions. These buses are likely double-deckers or have removable sunroofs, provide guided audio tours, and are typically quite expensive. If you are short on time, they may be worth the money. In Barcelona, for instance, we had only one very hot day to see the sights, and the hop-on, hop-off bus made it easy to go from one end of town to the other without worrying about train schedules or how far we might have to walk in the sun.

FINDING FOOD

Even at home, finding healthy food that your kids will eat is a challenge. On the road, you'll face the same battles. Hopefully your kids have tried or are excited to try at least some foods that they will encounter on your trip. On short trips, you might let nutrition slide. On longer adventures, you'll need to worry about whether they're eating enough protein, whether they're eating way too much sugar, and whether a fruit or vegetable has passed their lips. Most countries have traditional foods that incorporate either noodles or rice so carbohydrates are rarely difficult. New fruits and vegetables are always fun to try, even if you have to cajole your kids and they don't taste as good as you hope. In some less-developed countries, you'll need to be careful of raw fruits and vegetables because of sanitization or fertilization methods. In some countries, actually finding a fruit or vegetable on a menu can be an obstacle.

Obviously you can find food in a new country at restaurants. These run the gamut from expensive and formal to inexpensive temporary stalls in the street. If

MAKE A MEAL

Making at least one meal on your own on the road is really a neat experience, even if it's only a picnic. Visit the grocery store or the market (or both) to find out what everyone else is eating. Browse all the aisles. What is the most common grain? What seem to be the staple foods? Can you assemble the ingredients for one family meal? Is there enough precooked or easy-to-eat food to make a picnic? Check out the produce, the meats, the snacks, and the desserts. What kind of kid drinks do they sell? How many can you sample over the course of your stay? If you have a night or two in an apartment with a kitchen, try cooking an entire dinner.

you are like us, you will want to explore a wide variety of choices while avoiding places with questionable hygiene and saving fancy places for really special occasions. Most places will be happy to see your family and many have special meals just for kids. Almost any restaurant can whip up either plain noodles or rice (depending on the continent). Even though child etiquette varies widely, it has been the rare occurrence where we sensed that we were out of place getting out crayons as entertainment until the food arrived.

Another great place to find food is at the local market. Whether at a grocery store or a farmer's market, you can glimpse into the culture of the country you are visiting. Just seeing what products are available in grocery stores is often interesting. In many places people shop for food on a daily basis, rather than loading up the trunk with two weeks of food at Costco. Just go to a grocery store and wander the aisles. Is it surprising that mustard comes in a tube? Are there many kinds of meat and cheese? Exotic vegetables? Rows and rows of pickled goods or fifty kinds of rice? Farmer's markets are even more enlightening, since you interact with the people who produce the food. At a market, you will have direct access to fresh fruit and vegetables that you might not be able to find so readily in restaurants. (See "Make a Meal.")

If you have special dietary restrictions or allergies, plan ahead! You can't think very well when you're starving. For each country, prepare a slip of paper written in the native language explaining your situation. People will be ready to help if they can clearly understand what you need.

Breakfast

Continental breakfasts are sometimes included in the cost of hotel rooms. Although the food offerings can be unpredictable, varying from hot entrées to stale rolls, breakfast in-house saves the time and energy of looking for food first thing in the morning. Be aware that the quality of the breakfast is not necessarily related to the quality or cost of the hotel. We've had some awful breakfasts in some nice hotels and vice versa. If you have access to a refrigerator, take advantage of the local markets and store your preferred breakfast foods overnight. If you have no way of storing the food, one person can get up early and pick up breakfast at the market. Of course there are always restaurants, but we've generally found that going out for breakfast every day is expensive and time-consuming.

Lunch

Lunch is the easiest meal because there are so many possibilities. We try to do it differently every day. If we have leftovers or if we're staying in an apartment with a kitchen, we may pack a hearty picnic and eat in a park, at the beach, or in a museum café (see "Make a Meal"). It's cheap and you can be sure to have exactly the kid food you need. Sometimes we dine at a local market. Often markets are best midday and you can finally get some fresh fruit and vegetables into your kids (choose wisely depending on sanitation). It's usually cheap and a great

---

INFANT TIP: NURSING ON THE ROAD

- It's a lot easier to nurse in a foreign country than it will be to feed a toddler. At that age you'll need bits of food, clean hands, and a place to prepare meals, so enjoy the simplicity.
- As baby's schedule adjusts, he'll nurse at somewhat different times of the day. Milk production will adjust accordingly.
- If you're using bottles, pack spares. Keep spare bottles, bags, and formula in your carry on. Luggage gets lost, flights get delayed, but babies still need to eat!
- If you want a glass of wine while traveling, you can test your milk for alcohol using Milkscreen (milkscreen.com), a portable test strip that tells you whether your breastmilk is safe. It's tiny and easy to pack.
- For pumping on the road, bring spare tiny parts and keep them separately in your luggage. When you leave your pump all clean and disassembled on a hotel towel, it's easy for bits to get lost. Lost pump parts are a big bummer.
- Patience, confidence, flexibility, and spare parts...pretty much all you need for happy babies on the road!

MEALTIME IS FAMILY TIME: A DOZEN GAMES FOR THE TABLE

Here are some ideas for games to play while you are waiting for your food to arrive, for your bus to depart, or whenever you have some time to kill and want to keep your older kids engaged.

1. **Animal Alphabet Link:** Start with any animal. The next person has to name an animal that starts with the last letter of that animal. The next person has to name an animal that starts with the last letter of the second animal. Goat, tadpole, elephant…

2. **Acronym Insanity:** One person comes up with a phrase in their head and then says its acronym out loud. Go around in a circle and try to guess what the acronym stands for. You can add a theme like "menu entrée descriptions" or "common things Dad says." Example, "ITS" stands for "Isn't That Something."

3. **Famous Initials:** Think of a famous person and say their initials. Go around and try to guess. The first person to guess correctly starts the next round.

4. **Initial Madness:** Think of a common phrase about twenty letters long (for example, "The tail wags the dog"). On a big napkin, write down the first ten letters and then write the second ten letters underneath. You now have a set of ten sort-of random initials (the top letter goes with the bottom letter). Everyone writes down as many famous people as they can think of with those initials (you can also add people you all know) for one minute. Then go around and say one famous person out loud at a time, if anyone else has that person, you cross it off all the lists. At the end, count up the number of correct names each person has remaining.

5. **FamPic:** The first person draws a line, without lifting the pencil, while the next person counts to ten. Pass the drawing on so that each family member draws, without lifting the pencil, for the count of ten. Then go around the table taking turns describing your work of art.

6. **Caption This!:** Pull out the digital camera and let the first person pick one photo. Each family member gets ten seconds to look at the photo. Next everyone dreams up a funny caption. Take turns sharing the captions for that photo as you display it again.

7. **I'm Going on a Picnic: Riddle Version:** One person, the host, picks a secret category or rule to which all players must adhere (such as all answers must be something red). Next, they say 'I'm going on a picnic

and I'm bringing _____ [filling in the blank with something that fits their rule]. What do you want to bring?" The next person, in an attempt to guess the rule, replies "I'm going on a picnic and I'm bringing _____?" The host either says "yes, you can bring it" or "nope, sorry, you can't come," based on whether the player picked an answer that fit their rule. Of course replies can get more creative or even rude as you get sillier or hungrier. Go around listening to each answer and trying to guess the rule. You never say the rule out loud, you just always guess something that you can bring until it's obvious everyone knows the rule (or until the youngest gets frustrated or your food arrives). Possible rules: 1) accepted items have to occur in alphabetical order—something beginning with "a," then "b," then "c"…; 2) begins with the first letter of the player's name (note that Zoey will not be allowed to bring the same items as Logan); 3) begins with the last letter of the player's name; 4) begins with the last letter of the item that was just 'brought to the picnic' (this is a hard one!); 5) an item that is the color of the shirt you are wearing (also amazingly tough). You can go easier like, it must have an "o" in it or it has to be a spherical item. And there are super easy rules for really young kids such as items that start with "a", are a particular color, or are a fruit. Make up your own rule.

8. **I'm Going on a Picnic: Memory Version:** Starts the same way: 'I'm going on a picnic and I'm bringing _____," but instead of guessing the rule, the next person has to repeat what the first person said and add an item. The third person has to repeat what the first two people said and then add another item. Keep going around until no one can remember the whole chain.

9. **I'm Going on a Picnic: Tongue Twister Version:** Starts the same way but the first example has to be five words that all begin with "a." The next person gets "b" and then "c" and so on. So the first person might say "Anxious albino alligators and almonds" and the second person could say "Baby blue beluga barfing berries." Some letters are pretty challenging.

10. **Two Truths and a Lie:** Take turns stating three "facts" about yourself. Two of them should be true and one of them false. Family members vote on which they think is the lie.

11. **Fact or Fiction:** The first person tells a story and then everyone guesses whether it was fact or fiction. If you guess right, you get a point. The storyteller gets a point for each person tricked. Try to get the most points

before dinner arrives by tricking everyone when you tell your story and by seeing through everyone else's tales.

12. **Pancakes:** One person is It. The other family members go around in a circle and ask him or her any question they want and the only answer can be "pancake" but the person who is It cannot laugh. Whoever makes him or her laugh first, becomes It. The person who just laughed can name a new word to substitute for "pancake" in the next round.

local experience. There are lunch restaurants but they often waste good midday time, cost more than they should, and generally involve too much sitting still and waiting during an active time of the day. Lunch in a fancy restaurant can be a big treat, however. A trick we learned from Bill's parents is to go to the super-fancy restaurant for lunch; you get the same food, same chef, portions that are more manageable, a more kid-friendly atmosphere, and—best of all—half to two-thirds the price! Although we do take our kids to fancy restaurants at night on occasion, we dread the possibility of breaking up someone else's romantic evening with our cheerios and singing.

Dinner

Dinner is when we try to relax, chat, and slow down. We prefer local restaurants away from the tourist centers; they tend to be cheaper and more authentic. But the possibilities will depend on where you're staying, if you're up for another walk or taxi ride, and where you're traveling. Sometimes you're stuck with overpriced tourist food. Make the best of it.

We never land at dinner without some activities. Sometimes we let the kids read their books, sometimes we bring postcards, sketch pads, or journals. We often play games (see "Mealtime Is Family Time") or ask questions like, "What was your favorite part of the day?" or, "If you lived in this city, where would you build your house?" And while I know many a waiter frowned at us, we brought snacks into restaurants when the kids were young in case the kids couldn't manage anything on the menu but plain rice or noodles.

Snacks

With toddlers and babies, we carried oodles of baggies of bites: Cheerios, cut grapes, yogurt in a tube, and so on. Even once our kids were old enough to survive on three meals a day, we didn't stop bringing snacks. Snacks are good; healthy snacks are brilliant. They take the pressure off mealtime, stave off evil temper fits, and entertain. A bag of crackers and a few servings of fruit are easy to take with you everywhere.

We also carry high-protein energy bars everywhere, always. It's like having a restaurant in your day bag. Energy bars are a lot of calories so we don't eat them every day. But when you are still ten blocks from the museum and someone starts melting down, you need protein and you need it quickly even if it is packed with sugar. Energy bars can even be doled out at restaurants when the only menu items the kids will touch are just grease and starch. In developed countries, we've found that you can buy energy bars on the road. In less developed countries, we bring two or three per person per week, just in case.

SECURING SHELTER

For nights where you haven't prearranged your lodging, you will need to find an appropriate place to sleep. This will probably take time and effort—be sure that you have budgeted for both. To find shelter on the fly with children in tow there should be abundant lodging options, or at least some high degree of lodging reliability so you don't find yourself out in the cold (maybe literally). Sometimes we bring the kids and ask to look at a room in each of two or three hotels. Then we let the kids choose which room they like best. Another effective system is to divide the duties between the parents—one parent is in charge of the kids while the other is in charge of finding the lodging. Sometimes one parent/child team goes in search of lodging while the other team enjoys a bit of extra museum or relaxation time. Each team has to agree up front to trust the other's judgment. No one appreciates criticism at the end of a long day. On an off-season trip to a small beach town in northern Spain, one of us hung out with the kids on the beach (not a hard job) while the other roamed the pretty streets looking at rooms in the few hotels that were open (also not a hard job). We ended up in maybe the best cheap room in town. It had an in-room spiral staircase, a pink couch, and a terrific view. We never would have found this room on the internet in advance.

In most airports and transportation stations there are tourist offices that can help with the search for lodging, but be wary of for-profit tourist advice. Some tourist information booths are just small businesses that survive on commissions from various hotels, restaurants, and tour groups in town. Travel books can list some good deals too, but we've found that recommendations in popular books can flood hotels or guesthouses with eager tourists and destroy the authentic, local atmosphere. Even if the lodging comes highly recommended from a tourist information booth or a guidebook, it's a prudent strategy to check out the room before committing.

FAMILY LIFE ON THE LOOSE

Every day will be a little different on your travel adventure. Variety is part of the excitement of the journey. In fact, it's probably a big reason why you are on the journey in the first place. But the constant change can also be challenging. Be ready to share choices, define expectations to your kids in advance, and help them stay safe in new environments. On the road, you'll enjoy more uninterrupted family time than you find at home. As a family, you'll be navigating, foraging, and finding shelter. These basics are fun and integral parts of your trip. Next, we'll delve into the educational rewards of your travel experience: learning about the country and culture that now surrounds you.

CITY SCAVENGER HUNT

The following three-page scavenger hunt is as generic as possible. Your kids should be able to use it in almost any urban city. You could even try it in several cities and compare your results. Points can be assigned if you want individuals in the family to compete.

- Copy pages in advance or let your kids fill in the example in the book.
- Sheets can be photocopied directly, cut to a smaller size, filled in during the day, and taped into a travel journal.
- To expand these sheets to a full 8 ½ by 11 page, photocopy at 121%, a standard pre-set on many photocopy machines. Younger kids will likely do better with the expanded sheets, which allow more room for writing and drawing.
- A wise parent will guide their child to sketch a manhole cover that is next to a café or near a sunny park bench!

If your family enjoys this scavenger hunt, try making your own. You can send us yours at info@familyontheloose.com. City-specific scavenger hunts will appear on our website, familyontheloose.com, as we receive and create them.

City _____ Country _____ Date _____

City Scavenger Hunt

The number in the black circle shows how many points each activity is worth.

Draw or describe one major icon.

(20)

Use a map and sketch the general layout of your location.

(20)

10+

Fill in the name of a famous... Check the box if you saw it! Each item is worth ten points.

street _____ ☐

bridge _____ ☐

museum _____ ☐

statue _____ ☐

department store _____ ☐

building _____ ☐

historical figure _____ ☐

district _____ ☐

10+

In this city, I got around by... (Check as many as possible—ten points each)

☐ foot   ☐ train   ☐ subway   ☐ tram   ☐ bus   ☐ funicular

☐ cable car ☐ bike   ☐ boat   ☐ taxi   ☐ car   ☐ horse

☐ other _____   ☐ other _____

City _____ Country _____ Date _____

City Scavenger Hunt

Find the following and draw or describe where you found it in the box.

10	**10**	**10**
dome	small path or trail	grocery store or market
10	**10**	**10**
cross	unusual window	big tree
10	**10**	**10**
hexagon	star	umbrella

Draw one funny advertisement and record the slogan.

10

City _____ Country _____ Date _____

City Scavenger Hunt

Sketch a manhole cover!

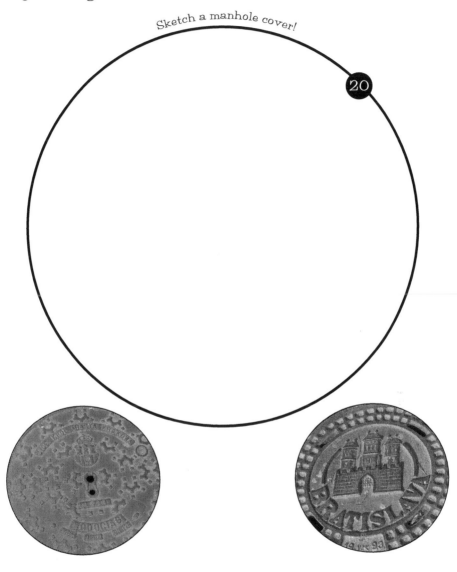

20

Tally up your points for each day of the scavenger hunt.

Day 1 _____ Day 2 _____ Total _____

6 Learning as You Go

Taking a trip to any place new will be a learning experience for everyone in your family, but it is also a unique opportunity to incorporate traditional academic topics into the cross-cultural educational experience. We've already talked about learning some of the language, history, geography, and culture of your destination during trip preparation, and this learning will no doubt continue and be reinforced while you are on your adventure. But in this chapter we discuss how to enrich the museum, the market, and even the beach by nudging your kids to write, think, draw, and listen. These ideas are designed not only to be educational tools, but also to engage your kids in your travel experience by providing a helpful structure. We present strategies we have used to keep our children interested in experiencing many new places.

VISIT A MUSEUM

When thinking about kids and museums, most people conjure up images of the children's museum, a science museum, or a natural history museum. All of these are fun and great examples can be found all over the world. There are also open-air museums, ancient houses, and toy museums lurking in or near many major cities. But when thinking about visiting Paris, Florence, or New York, the Louvre, the Uffizi, and the Met are likely the museums that come to mind. Unfortunately, these aren't usually high on kids' lists of must-see attractions. So how do you manage to get into and through the great museums of the world with children in tow? Preparation, planning, and patience.

First of all, acknowledge that many museums are just too big for one visit. The length of time needed to see everything in a big museum is just not feasible with children. If you get one to three hours out of the kids in one visit to a museum, consider it a success. Do not expect to see everything! One way to make a museum trip last longer and be more engaging is to prepare the kids well in advance. Show pictures of what they will see in the museum. Read stories about the famous paintings, sculptures, or artists. You can also approach the museum from your kids' perspective. Which exhibits have images of animals, sports, soldiers, ballerinas, or ancient weaponry?

Another way to streamline a museum visit is by avoiding the lines that zap energy from even the most enthusiastic young art fan. You can make reservations ahead of time online at some museums in order to bypass the ticket line when you arrive. Check the internet before you leave home, since famous museums tend to sell out their quota of reserved tickets weeks beforehand. Some museums have children's lines that allow family access to the museum faster than the central line. These museums acknowledge the limited concentration span of young viewers or the vulnerability of kids standing in a long line in ninety-degree heat.

Once you are inside, let the kids have a say in what to see. Another gallery of Renaissance paintings may not be as interesting as a room full of mummies, but maybe you can route yourselves through the Renaissance room on the way to the Egyptian section. You can even start in the gift shop if you are brave enough, and let them select postcards of three paintings they want to see, or they can browse the gifts related to particular exhibits. Best of all, give your child an activity sheet that guides them to draw, question, compare, and read (see "Museum Activity Sheets!" and the activity sheets section at the back of this chapter). Check if the museum has organized kid activities or materials.

MANAGE A SOUVENIR BUDGET

Everybody likes to buy stuff when they are traveling and your kids will be drawn like magnets to every souvenir stand on the planet. If your kids happen to miss a shopping opportunity, they needn't fret—it will likely come to them. Vendors in most countries are pretty wise to the ways of extricating cash from your wallet by marketing to your kids. Instead of saying "no," "No," and finally "NO!" give them a budget and let them make their own decisions. In chapter two we discussed helping kids plan and budget in advance of the trip. Now they can put all that planning to work. There will be many parts of the trip that, try as you might, you simply can't let the kids make the decisions. So let them have full control over something—their own spending.

Older kids can handle a trip-scale budget. Talk in advance about any super-compelling spending opportunities and small town versus metropolis prices, and then give them an estimated budget per destination. For example, you

MUSEUM ACTIVITY SHEETS!

Worksheets get a bad rap because of uninspired overuse. Students have been subjected to mindless busy-work for decades first via the mimeograph machine, then Xerox, and now classroom printers. But before we throw the baby out with the bathwater, we should wonder how worksheets ever developed into an unrivaled phenomenon of the twenty-first century elementary and middle school classroom. In the beginning, teachers were trying to keep kids engaged by involving them in the activity and giving them focus. Teachers wanted kids to know what to do without having to tell them. And kids love activity sheets because the sheets focus their attention on a specific task. Put a clipboard and a scavenger hunt in the hands of an eight-year-old in a museum and—*voilà*—they know where to concentrate and what to do. They have an idea of how long they will be staying and they have autonomy. They also have a customized, self-guided museum tour. Copy the museum activity sheets at the back of this chapter or make some yourself designed specifically for your children's ages, interests and the displays you plan to visit.

Well-considered activity sheets are your ticket to relaxation. Mete them out mindfully for special occasions and you have cheap, enriching childcare. Overuse them and their ability to engage and amuse your children will evaporate.

might be visiting two countries with a total of five destinations, but only one is a big city. You could give your fourteen-year-old son a $100 travel budget and note that it comes to about $20 per destination. You might want to go through the itinerary and note that there is a craft market in one village and another village is famous for metalwork. The city prices will likely be higher but the only traditional souvenirs will likely be in the city. If you hear, "Dad, pleeease can I stop for a pack of gum?" the minute you pass the first airport newsstand, mention that the same cash might buy a nifty quartz rock or a small clay animal sculpture at your destination. Then, let him decide. For younger kids or less experienced travelers, a budget by destination is probably better. You don't want them to blow the whole budget at the first stop or save every penny until the last town where there is nothing to buy but lace doilies.

Want to sneak a little math or accounting into the trip? Encourage your kids to track their budget in writing. Revisit the budget resources from chapter two. The "Sample Souvenir Budget Worksheet," can be photocopied or modified and kept in their journal. Your kids will need to convert currency and they can even graph how they spend their money over time. If you track it in writing, your kids don't have to carry around cash and you don't have to keep their change separate from your own. This is especially helpful if you will be traveling through multiple currencies because you don't want them to lose money converting in each destination.

We've started giving trip spending money as birthday and holiday presents. The kids enjoy spending as they choose and we are off the hook for involving parents in decisions about trip trinkets.

ENJOY LOCAL MUSIC

Most remember to take their kids to art museums, historical landmarks, and famous icons. But what about music? Music differs all over the world, it's everywhere, and listening is often free. You may encounter local outdoor concerts, special cultural events, and street performers. It can be difficult to explore the full range of musical possibility before you go, so take advantage of being on the road to expand your child's understanding of music in its many forms.

Street musicians are in nearly every tourist destination around the world and many are quite talented. Stop and enjoy music on the road during your next trip. Street musicians gather in fairly predictable places so track them down when you have time to relax and enjoy the performance. Discuss with your kids the

ENDLESS MATH GAME

Our friend's mother was a math teacher and she taught us the world's best travel math game. You can play it while you walk, in a bus, at night, or over a hot chocolate. Ask for four single digit numbers (a mix of odd and even numbers works best) and one double digit number. Now use any mathematical operators to make the four single digit numbers equal the double digit number. For example, use 3, 4, 6, 7, and 14. One answer is: $((3 \times 4)/6) \times 7 = 14$. It can be challenging! For younger kids, stick to low double digit numbers. As kids get older, you can add exponents, square roots, and higher double digit numbers. Experiment with modifications of the game such as starting with only three single digit numbers or trying to reach a triple digit number. Pick one double digit number and test as many different sets of four single digits as you can. Are any of the sets impossible? Is it easier to make equations that equal odd numbers or even numbers? Need help choosing numbers? Choose the first numeral on each of the next four license plates you pass or use the digits of the next phone number you see on an advertisement.

instruments, the musical selection, and any cultural nuances. Let them dance or sit back and act cool (depending on their age). We saw a street performer in Prague playing amplified water glasses—awesome! And in that same city there are hourly trumpet calls in the town square, operas, chamber quartets, and even bands announcing the changing of the palace guard.

Where else can you find music? Church services often include beautiful music, temples might have chanting monks, and restaurants may provide live performances. Local concerts are usually posted on community bulletin boards, announced in the local paper, or listed online. If you don't speak the language, a local might be able to help you figure out what is available. There are landmarks of famous composers or musicians to visit, and even music museums like the Haus der Musik in Vienna. Countries, and sometimes regions within countries, may have a special local instrument that your kids can try, such as a didgeridoo in Australia, the klong thap in Thailand, or a kalimba gourd thumb piano from Burkina Faso. Surf YouTube for short videos demonstrating these instruments before you go—or after you purchase one as a souvenir.

Most theatrical or cultural performances include music. Movies from or about your destination often include local music in the soundtrack. Ask your kids about the music. How is it different from pop music at home? What adjectives would you use to describe it? How is music different from east to west? From country to city? Is music integrated into daily life differently in different cultures? Some locations lend themselves to a sound journal (see chapter seven, "The World's Best Travel Journal") or to a collection of quick sound samples. Local music CDs can be a fantastic and compact souvenir, especially for older kids. Teens can collect pop music from around the world. To save space, music can be burned to your laptop and the physical CDs left behind (don't forget to back up your music and any other files to a USB drive that you keep in a separate bag or to a cloud drive). Where there are no CDs, ask to take a video of a song or street performance.

EXPLORE THE LOCAL LIFE

Of course you are going to visit museums, icons like the Eiffel Tower and the

TRAVEL TIP: SELL ART IN THE PARK

Take your kids, portable paints, charcoal pencils, or nice colored pencils, a huge sketchpad, and plenty of snacks to the park for an afternoon. If you can find a park with other working artists, let your kids observe the artists at work for a few minutes. Then set your kids loose to create a small gallery. As they paint or sketch each masterpiece, they can lay it out on a bench or on the sidewalk and price it to sell.

Taj Mahal, castles, ruins, and other famous tourist destinations, but save time to explore local life. Bring a sketchpad to a café and encourage your child to draw while you do a little people watching, browse a guidebook, or chat with other adults. Spend an hour at a park with a playground. You can find the coolest play structures by "flying" around with Google Earth near to where you are staying.

Public swimming pools can also be major cultural immersion experiences. In Thailand, Ashley was instructed not to drop her towel and bare her bathing suit-clad body until she was right next to the water. In Austria, the changing rooms and even some showers are co-ed. Maybe visiting the Olympic swimming pool with a view of Barcelona is not quite as classically cultural as a guided tour of the minor sculptures of the Sagrada Família, but everyone can use a break from the beaten path.

Want to really discover local life? Send your family on a traditional scavenger hunt one afternoon. You can split up into two teams, go around all together, or let older kids go out on their own. Create a list of seemingly common, everyday items: toothpicks, nail clippers, salt, socks, a spoon, leaf, playing cards, tea, gum,

TRAVEL TIP: HAND OVER THE CAMERA

Waiting for a bus, a train, a dinner reservation, or a friend can bring on the boredom that spells meltdown. Try passing over the digital camera to your kids! They'll have a lot of fun being in charge of the camera, either taking or reviewing pictures. Young kids should keep the strap around their neck and may need a little help keeping themselves and your camera safe. Older kids might already have their own camera so now is the time to give them an "assignment." Ask them to create a self-portrait that really shows how bored they are or that demonstrates what they were thinking about on this particular day. You might also charge them with taking a series of local portraits, as kids may be less embarrassed about pointing the camera at people; teach them to ask first, even if you have a super-zoom lens. Other fun assignments might include taking a series of pictures of street life, sculptures, as many different types of faces as possible, or advertising that you would never see at home. For the oldest kids, give them journalistic challenges such as: three pictures that define the culture you are visiting; five pictures in which you can (or can't) tell what country you are visiting; a picture that expresses a particular emotion such as happiness, disappointment, or hope; or a still life of objects found in nature. Many of these photos will make a wonderful addition to their travel journal, travel blog, or the family photo book.

dice. Modify the list depending our your locale, but pick things that would be simple to find at home, that will be found in different types of stores or markets, that are cheap and small, and that might come in handy on your trip. Give a copy of the list to each team, offer a $10 budget, and set them loose! At the end of the hunt, each team gets one point for every item they found on the list. Compare stories, successes, and surprises over dinner. (A handy tip: if you can find dice, your kids can design handmade board games about your location. See "Make Your Own Board Game.")

Browsing is fun too. Local bookstores or libraries are essential stops for us—we like to browse children's books in other languages or seek out a book (in English) by a local author or a fiction book set in our location. Our kids really enjoy browsing stationary stores (pads of paper, pens, colored pencils, erasers) in every country and there isn't much that's quite as fun as shopping for candy in a foreign land. You might also consider visiting a local school (you may have to ask for permission in advance), university, movie theater, or shopping mall.

LEARN ABOUT LOCAL HISTORY

No matter how much your family was able to learn before you embarked on your journey, nothing brings history to heart like being on-site (see "Create a Timeline"). Most places carry some of their history on their sleeve: in their museums, their historic buildings, and

MAKE YOUR OWN BOARD GAME

With a thick piece of paper and a pen, your kids can create a board game set in your location. For younger kids, you can make the game a version of chutes and ladders with some squares sending you backward and some squares sending you forward. These should all be location and travel themed successes and setbacks. Forward squares might include, "Taken to the front of the line at the Louvre!" or, "Discover the secret of the designs on Buddha's feet." Backwards slides might read, "Pick-pocketed," "Crowd so big at the changing of the guard that you can't see anything," or, "Rains on your hike." As kids get older, they can add disaster cards at certain spots, jail, trivia questions, and much more. Can they set the game in a relevant historical epoch? Who will the players be (objects as in Monopoly or fictional characters as in Clue)? The game board can be decorated with markers or colored pencils when it is first created or during dull travel moments. The game itself can be played on the train or as you wait for dinner to be served.

CREATE A TIMELINE

Most cultures are much older than our typical North American culture, where "old" can be defined as a few decades and a century is positively ancient. Keeping the dates of major historical events straight can be confusing, even for a history major. A great visual tool for representing relationships between historical events is a timeline. A timeline displays events chronologically and will make it easy to see why Napoleon did not bump into Picasso. A timeline can also show how major historic events depend on previous events. For example, Napoleon helped to unite small states into Germany, which later sided with Austria-Hungary in escalating a political assassination into World War I. Depending on where you are going, you could also include reference points that are already familiar to your kids (their birthday, when your own home was built, Lewis and Clark's expedition, or Columbus coming to America) to demonstrate how relatively young recorded North American history is compared to a lot of the rest of the world. As you travel, keep the timeline going, adding dates as you learn more about where you are. How old is the hotel? When was that famous painting painted? You'll probably need a long, skinny piece of paper or a scroll. Receipt tape from an office supply store works great. Store it in a toilet paper tube!

in their culture. Just walking down the street of an old city will contextualize what you tried to learn before you left home. And now that you are here, learning the details of the history will be so much easier than learning esoteric facts from afar. Your kids will want to know about the knights and princesses that slept in the castle on the hill above your hotel because they don't have to imagine the details of the place; they can look out the window.

TAKE A HIKE!

Do your kids need a chance to simply burn off some energy? Climb! There are more things to climb that you might first imagine: hillsides with beautiful views, church steeples, old parts of town, castle ruins, lookout towers, and temple stairs. A good climb is a great way to enjoy something special with your kids, exercise, and explore a not-too-touristy (maybe) local attraction. In hiking, bribery can be a valuable parenting tool. Pick out a bag of candy or other treat and agree to enjoy it at the top. If you can find something with interesting stairs to climb (for example, very old steps that are spiral), all the better. Plan your climb to coincide with a cooler part of the day and at the time your kids might most need some unstructured energy release. We've had fun counting steps and even betting on how many steps there will be. The person who guesses the number of steps most closely without going over wins the first piece of candy or chooses the dinner venue.

In many areas, there are hikes or long walks that can interest the whole family. Look for nature parks or local greenways. Sometimes well-known tourist attractions can be approached by foot instead of tour bus. Even large, semi-urban parks can provide several miles of interesting outdoor walking. Since these excursions are generally free of charge, they are rarely advertised so a bit of advance internet or local guidebook research is usually required. Once out in the woods, take advantage of the chance to compare ecosystems, flora and fauna, and local attitudes about wilderness. In Korea, Ashley hiked several miles into a national park to find a café seemingly in the middle of nowhere—a fun surprise. Even more interesting, the café was full of nicely dressed women in high heels. Ashley had seen a few of these women on the path but hadn't known what to make of the phenomena. Apparently, three-inch stilettos were all the rage in backcountry footgear at the time.

Providing structure to your hike can really help things go smoothly. Adding a little cross-cultural, cross-ecological education to your adventure is always fun too. Here are some ideas for activities to enrich an outdoor hike:

- As they hike, ask your kids to come up with five ways the relationship between humans and nature is different in this country and then have a post-hike debrief. They might consider interpretive signs, the presence or absence of public transportation, clothing, which segment of the population seems to be enjoying the outdoors, how parents interact with children, and when or where people eat.
- Make a list of new and different life forms that you observe along the way. Ecologically curious older artists can record plants with simple sketches. For

TRAVEL TIP: PAINTING ROCKS

Hanging out by a rocky beach or trying to relax in a park? Buy a cheap set of watercolor paints and have your kids paint rocks. They can create a museum display in a corner of the park, hide surprise rock art in crevices between big rocks, or lay out an art path on the beach. Make sure to explain that the paint will wash off in the next rainstorm or high tide so your temporary displays will not deface the park or mar the natural beauty of the beach for others. Take lots of photographs before the art vanishes.

younger kids, insects are really fun. Draw your discoveries since you probably won't be able to identify them by name. In the tropics, recording all the species you observe on a three-mile hike would be equivalent to writing a Ph.D. dissertation. In some other areas, you might find only a few species in a mile.

- Allow time for your child to sketch the view from the top of the hike with a small sketchpad and a set of colored pencils.
- Pick up a little animal statue or a set of figurines before the hike. Have one parent run ahead and hide the treasures along the path. The kids can search as they hike. After they locate the little figures, they can run ahead and hide them for the parents or each other.
- Make a map of your hike. The level of detail depends on your child's age and interest level, but identifying unique and map-able attributes is the real fun. Is this tree grove worth putting on the map? What should we call this resting ledge?
- Give your kids a photographic assignment. They might record the differences in vegetation as elevation changes, or take a set of five wildflower photos that could be made into sets of greeting cards (great holiday gifts for family!). Capture examples of human influence in the wilderness or park. Use photos to describe the habitat of one of the charismatic regional animals.

EDUCATION IS EVERYWHERE

In this chapter, we've offered just a few of the endless ways to creatively incorporate education into your family adventure. Any place you are spending time can be turned into a *de facto* classroom: the hotel room, the restaurant table, or the train seat. The subjects you cover can vary with your family's interests: math with currency or metric system conversion, geography with maps and planning the daily route, or science with weather forecasting or ecosystem exploration. Although culture, language, and history are infused into everything you'll do and see on the road, these subjects can also be highlighted and explored in more depth. In the next chapter, we delve into journaling as a way to enrich what the kids are learning on the road and preserve their memories for the future.

MUSEUM ACTIVITY SHEETS

The following pages are examples of museum activity sheets.

- These sheets are generally organized in order of sophistication. Younger kids will do best with the first sheets. Older kids might prefer the later sheets.
- The activity sheets are designed for use in a range of museums. Some will work better in an art museum while others lend themselves to other types of museums. Select ones that best fit your destination.
- Copy them in advance or let your kids fill in the example in the book. We sometimes copy two different pages to make a double-sided activity sheet.
- Sheets can be photocopied directly, cut to a smaller size, filled in at the museum, and taped into a travel journal.
- To expand these sheets to a full 8 ½ by 11 page, photocopy at 121%, a standard pre-set on many photocopy machines. Younger kids will likely do better with the expanded sheets, which allow more room for writing and drawing.
- We bring a clipboard or magazine as a hard surface to write on and colored pencils to draw with when we expect the kids to be filling out these activity sheets.

Check our website, familyontheloose.com, for more examples or try making your own. Send copies of your successful activity sheets, submit comments on ours, or provide ideas for more questions to include in future activity sheets to info@familyontheloose.com.

Museum _____ City_____ Date _____

Before you go in...

What's this museum famous for? _____
_____

Three things I really want to see:

1. _____

2. _____

3. _____

Two famous people associated with this museum:

1. _____

2. _____

Find something beginning with each of these letters:

B _____   N _____

C _____   P _____

D _____   Q _____

F _____   R _____

G _____   S _____

H _____   T _____

J _____   V _____

K _____   W _____

L _____   X _____

M _____   Z _____

Museum _____ City_____ Date _____

a. Make a detailed black and white sketch of one of your favorite items.

b. Name four of your details in the corner boxes and draw arrows to that part of the sketch.

1

2

3

4

Describe one object that has to do with:

medicine _____

law _____

science _____

business _____

sports _____

Museum _____ City _____ Date _____

Find the weirdest object on display. Sketch it.

If you could only show
your best friend one
thing, what would it
be and why?

_____

_____

_____

_____

_____

_____

_____

What is the coolest thing
in the whole museum?

_____

_____

Find a group of
people looking at a
display and eavesdrop
on them. What do you think
they are talking about?

_____

What language are they speaking?

_____

How do they know each other?

_____

Do you think they like
the museum?

_____

Museum _____ City_____ Date _____

Before you enter:

What do you think will be inside? _____

_____

Name three things you want to find (check the boxes after you find them).

1. _____ ☐

2. _____ ☐

3. _____ ☐

Once you're inside:

Find a picture you like. Draw it from a different perspective than the artist used.

What other perspective would be interesting?

_____

_____

What is the most surprising thing in the original picture?_____

_____

_____

Add one new detail to your picture that is only visible from this new perspective.

● ●

Find two portraits and draw them.

Which person would you rather visit?_____

Why? _____

_____

What is the same between the portraits?_____

_____

What is different?

_____

_____

Museum _____ City _____ Date _____

Find three works of art by the most famous artist at the museum. What are they and when were they created?

1. _____   _____

2. _____   _____

3. _____   _____

What is special about these three works of art? _____

_____

Find a landscape painting and sketch one detail of the scene.

Write a short story about how this detail ended up in the landscape.

_____

_____

_____

_____

_____

_____

_____

_____

_____

Museum _____ City_____ Date _____

Seek and Score: Find as many objects on this list as you can. Write a few details to prove you found the object. Total your points.

horse _____ 5

watch _____ 15

brush _____ 5

portrait _____ 10

tooth _____ 5

spoon _____ 10

radio _____ 15

mirror _____ 20

backpack _____ 10

lemon _____ 20

sunset _____ 15

water _____ 10

sword _____ 5

pocket knife _____ 10

dog _____ 10

fish _____ 5

tiger _____ 15

trophy _____ 20

artist _____ 20

mug _____ 10

caterpillar _____ 15

Subtotal _____

Museum _____ City_____ Date _____

Seek and Score continued...

Subtotal from previous page _____

deck of cards _____ 20

money _____ 5

box _____ 5

beet _____ 5

hammer _____ 15

glasses _____ 10

rat _____ 5

cupcake _____ 25

dice _____ 25

hat _____ 15

Total _____

Sketch the funniest two objects from the above list.

Find the signatures of four artists and copy them here.

1. _____ 2. _____

3. _____ 4. _____

Museum _____ City_____ Date _____

Find one exhibit that's not interesting at all. Stare at it for two minutes. Write
down ten words that came to mind.

_____   _____

_____   _____

_____   _____

_____   _____

_____   _____

Find one interesting thing. What is it?

_____

Make it the subject of a cartoon strip.

Title _____

Find a room of art with titles. Wander, look, and dream up new titles for each
art object. Write down the old and new titles for the best one you invented.

Old title

_____

_____

New title

_____

_____

Sketch it!

Museum _____ City _____ Date _____

Before you enter: what time periods do you think are on display in this musuem? If there might be an item from a time period below, check the box. Once you go in: Try to find and record one item from each checked box. Any surprises?

☐ 1920s _____   ☐ Medieval times _____

☐ Roman times _____   ☐ Ancient Egypt _____

☐ Rennaissance _____   ☐ Early 20th century _____

☐ 1980s _____   ☐ First World War _____

☐ Ice ages _____   ☐ 2012 _____

☐ Ancient Greece _____   ☐ 18th century _____

☐ 21st century _____   ☐ 1600s _____

☐ 1960s _____   ☐ Stone age _____

☐ 19th century _____   ☐ Prehistoric _____

Find one interesting object. Use colored pencils to make a sketch.

Find another object that is somehow related. Sketch it, too.

How are these objects related?

_____

What's strange about them?

_____

What's sad about them?

_____

Museum _____ City _____ Date _____

Draw a chronosequence (timeline) of objects that show change over time.

Year   Description

_____

_____

_____

_____

_____

_____

_____

_____

_____

_____

_____

_____

_____

_____

_____

_____

_____

_____

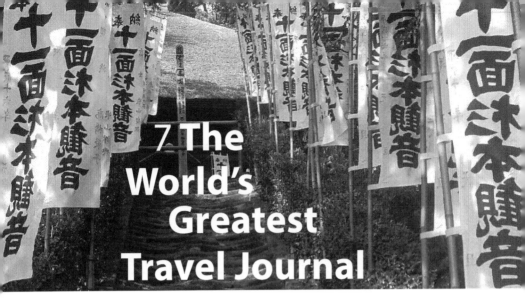

7 The World's Greatest Travel Journal

Keeping a journal can be a highlight of a journey for both young and old. It's a place to reflect on what you have seen; to be critical as well as complimentary; and to record new words, foods, sights, and even sounds. Traditionally, one thinks of the journal as a reflection of the trip. But it's worth turning this idea on its head: the trip experience—what your kids actually remember and absorb—can also be a function of how much they reflect and record in their journal. In our experience, the creativity and insight you apply to your adventure is directly related to your enjoyment of the journey. Your journal is the physical embodiment of that creativity and insight. If, for example, you spend some journal time detailing the similarities and differences between going to a restaurant in Seattle versus going to a restaurant in Vienna, your kids will naturally start observing the similarities and differences between going to a restaurant in Vienna versus Slovenia, and then in taking a bus in Seattle versus Vienna. The journal can help put the entire travel experience into context, and enable both memories and cultural lessons that will last a lifetime.

GET A GOOD JOURNALING BOOK

The first step in creating a journal is to acquire a nice blank book. If you are outrageously creative, you could make the book. But a journal can be subjected to some considerable wear and tear on a journey so think "rugged." Hard covers are great! In addition to words and pictures, the journal will eventually get filled with bits of this and bits of that—ticket stubs, maps, brochures, drawings done on napkins—and so a binding that can accommodate growth is a good choice. Spiral bindings allow you to draw or write on the left side of the page with ease or lay it open without getting frustrated by the cover slamming shut.

Bring your kids with you to pick out their journals! Barring a store trip, let them choose online or provide specifications. If you get a pink-covered journal for your eleven-year-old daughter who just outgrew all things girly, the odds of her pouring out her heart into it are slim to none. Your kids have to like their journal to want to write in it. Blank books of all types are generally available at bookstores, stationary stores, and some craft stores. Lab books from science supply catalogues or university bookstores are often designed for wear, spillage, and long-term use too.

If you are too strapped for time to buy a book, bring blank paper to assemble into a book when you get home. This isn't really such a bad idea for very long trips because as you tape in tickets stubs and postcards, journals tend to get large, bulky, and fragile. If you bring loose paper you can put away finished pages and protect them. Or you can photocopy the pages and send home the originals. You can even photograph each page with a digital camera and build a photo book out of the pages later. Our experience, however, is that kids like to write in a book, watching the pages fill up, and carrying it with them. There is something inspiring about a blank book: it motivates you to fill the empty pages and flip back through the completed pages. Remember, you don't need to do the same thing on every trip. Perhaps on the first trip, the kids need a blank book to get them started. But, on the second trip, they can visualize the completed project and they are inspired to try something new by building a journal with blank paper and a three-ring binder.

The tech-savvy may be inspired to create a digital journal or, perhaps, a website, blog, or wiki. A digital journal might be a neat alternative for a teenager who wants to perfect his computer skills or a family that doesn't want the extra weight of actual paper pages. Creating a blog and posting photos online is a super addition to any trip and a neat way to stay in touch with friends, family, and classrooms back home. However, the time involved is generally an order of magnitude greater than expected and it's not always an efficient or cost-effective use of those precious minutes in Copenhagen or Kathmandu. Also, the ability to work independently is essential for kids of all ages, especially older kids. If you decide on a digital journal or a blog, your kids will need independent internet access to make the project a success. Also consider that your child's journal is a private place for reflection. It's difficult to empty your head or your heart when you are aware that kids back home will be scrutinizing your words, your pictures, or your conclusions. And there will be customs, people, and places that your kids don't like. It's hard to write about things you don't like if it might hurt someone's feelings or produce resentment. So if you or your kid wants to blog, tweet, wiki, or upload, that's great, but perhaps the online record should be a supplement, not a replacement, for paper journals. We feel there really isn't a substitute for a private, paper journal that you can touch and hold. Especially for younger kids, the opportunity to draw with a crayon or pencil, to write private thoughts, and to tape in mementos is particularly fun and engaging.

When to Work on the Journal

It's really not possible to work on the journal at the same time every day because your schedule will vary. However, it's good to set the expectations that your child will do something in their journal regularly, and that quiet time will be used for working on the journal. You'll likely miss days and that's really no problem. But it's easier to negotiate with your kids when they say things like, "But I worked on it yesterday!" or, "I promise to do it tomorrow!" if you've set up their writing expectations in advance. Hopefully you won't end up with much whining and complaining in any case because of the variety of creative ideas we offer in this chapter. These ideas should help your child work independently and happily on their journal, with just a bit of participation from you.

It might work well to spend ten minutes on the journal every day before bedtime as an opportunity to wind down. We also like to work on our journals on trains and in restaurants. We keep the supplies (tape, scissors, pens, colored pencils, stickers, mementos) in a manila envelope and just carry it in our day bag. This solves two problems: finding the time to journal and keeping busy at potentially boring moments. If you enjoy a quiet drink or appetizers before dinner, this is an ideal time for your kids to write because you are available for questions but can also enjoy the peaceful minutes when they are engaged on their own.

What to Write in the Journal

Don't expect your kid to document your family's every move. In fact, unless your child happens to love this type of task, don't even encourage it. Look back at your own travel diaries. Ours can sometimes start with one day in painful detail, a few days with a few details, and then…blank pages. Why? Because documenting your every move is dull and tedious. Instead, the journal should be a place to reflect creatively. Vary it from day to day. One day you might chronicle the day's events and the next you might just tape in mementos and their descriptions. Things to do with your journal could include:

- Make a drawing instead of writing. You can draw the view from your hotel room, your favorite activity that day, or a picture of your family *en route*.
- Make a cartoon strip to show something funny that happened during the day.

- Collect receipts, ticket stubs, brochures, maps, business cards, restaurant logos, and more, and tape them into the journal.
- Make a collage of pictures cut from brochures.
- Make a map of that day's route. The map can explain your activities and remind you of the city layout.
- Tape in a tourist map that you highlighted with your route (see "Travel Tip: Everyone Likes a Map" in chapter five).
- Describe one character that you met that day—perhaps a funny man at a museum or a friendly child at the park. Write a short story about how they live and what kind of person you think they might be.
- Observe and discuss how parents treat their children. Is there a difference between this country and your home? What's the same? Add examples!
- Make a list of things you'd like to bring home with you. These could be works of art, food, ideas, phrases, or people. Then circle the ones you could actually take home.
- Describe the funniest thing that happened that day. The worst. The most boring. The most fun. The most surprising.
- Describe one meal that you really, really enjoyed.
- List ten things that are different and ten things that are similar about eating at a restaurant at home versus at your destination. You can expand this to many other comparisons between destinations.
- Reflect on a famous travel quotation (see "Quotations for Reflection").
- Describe the sounds you heard that day.
- If you are revisiting a place, how has the place changed? What do you see differently the second time around?
- Find a flower or new plant and make a very detailed sketch (to scale if possible) of the parts. If your child is an artist, she could end up with a fabulous collection of sketches at the end of the trip.
- Pick a very small architectural detail at a famous place—for example, a gargoyle. Sketch it or describe it in words. (This is also good for keeping engaged and busy at a museum.) If you need to move to a café or restaurant, take a photo of the detail so that your child can finish his sketch.
- Pick one tiny detail of a work of art and sketch it in the journal (again, a great museum activity). If this sort of activity really engages your child, go for a theme such as "dogs" or "umbrellas" or "toys" or "monsters."
- Tape in newspaper articles about current events or local culture.
- Let your kids interview you about your trip experiences. Record the interview in the journal.

QUOTATIONS FOR REFLECTION

Here are a few great quotations to use as jumping-off points for journal entries. Some of these are specifically about travel and culture while others are simply interesting. You could write a quotation into the journal for your child to reflect on. You can also copy these quotations onto small slips of paper, have your child select one at random, glue it in, and reflect. Often the randomness and the independence involved in the second method leads to interesting results. You might also use these (or others you find along the way) as dinner table conversation starters—a really good quotation should lead to an even better conversation.

- "A nation's culture resides in the hearts and in the soul of its people." —Mohandas Gandhi

- "From wonder into wonder existence opens." —Lao Tzu

- "For my part, I travel not to go anywhere, but to go. I travel for travel's sake. The great affair is to move." —Robert Louis Stevenson

- "Traveling is almost like talking with men of other centuries." —René Descartes

- "If you reject the food, ignore the customs, fear the religion and avoid the people, you might better stay at home." —James Michener

- "The world is a book and those who do not travel read only one page." —St. Augustine

- "A journey is best measured in friends, rather than miles." —Tim Cahill

- "All journeys have secret destinations of which the traveler is unaware." —Martin Buber

- "A traveler without observation is a bird without wings." —Moslih Eddin Saadi

- "Those who know nothing of foreign languages know nothing of their own." —Johann Wolfgang von Goethe

- "A good traveler has no fixed plans and is not intent on arriving." —Lao Tzu

- "A people without the knowledge of their past history, origin and culture is like a tree without roots." —Marcus Garvey

- "Journal writing is a voyage to the interior." —Christina Baldwin

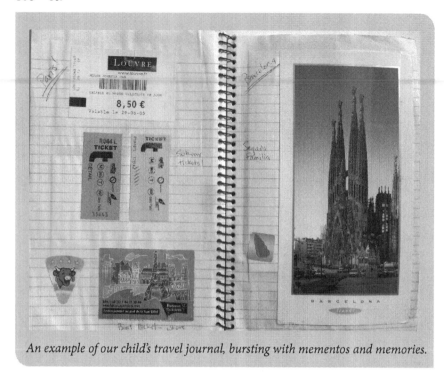

An example of our child's travel journal, bursting with mementos and memories.

SECRET QUESTIONS

Questions help everyone think and answering them inspires everyone to write. Try putting secret questions into your child's journal. You can do it while they sleep if the mystery might capture their attention or you can just give them a question off the top of your head when they sit down to write. A system that has worked well for us is to type up the questions in advance, cut them out, and stick them in an envelope in the back of the journal. When it's a "secret question day," your child can simply draw a question at random and tape it in.

Below are examples of questions that might help your child get started. You can photocopy and cut out the questions, or just skim them for ideas. The list is ordered from easier questions, aimed at younger kids, to harder questions for older kids, but you can mix it up to suit your own child's style. You should also add questions designed for your own kids or specialized to your destination. For example, ask questions about the rainforest when in Brazil or about Buddhism in Laos.

- Name three things today that surprised you.
- What are all the delicious foods you ate today?
- What things in this place remind you of stories you have read?

- Who are all the people you talked to today? Who was the most interesting?
- How is breakfast different in different countries or in different parts of the U.S.?
- How is dessert different in different countries?
- If your friend were planning a trip to visit this place, what would you tell them to do? What other advice would you give them?
- If you could be any of the famous historical figures we heard about today, who would you want to be? Why? What would you do differently?
- What was the most interesting fact you learned today and why did it impress you?
- What would your grandmother love about this place? What would she hate?
- Would it be fun to be here with your best friend from home? Why or why not?
- How is the history of this place reflected in what you saw today?
- Do religion and government seem to be separate here?
- In the U.S., people like to think that anyone can grow up to be President. Do people here seem to feel the same way? What evidence do you find that this is true or not true?
- How do the locals interact with nature? Is it similar or different to the way people at home interact with nature? What might drive those differences?
- What aspects of human nature are universal? What did you witness today to make you feel that way?
- How has this country's religion shaped its culture?
- How does the class system here compare to the class system at home? How do the rich and poor interact?
- What are the weather patterns like over the course of a year and how might this drive the local plant and animal communities?

JOURNAL LISTS

The journal is also a great place to keep records. Put the records or lists on a special page. Maybe you will record something every day or maybe only on selected days. Here are some ideas for interesting records your child might want to keep.

- The daily weather
- Cities visited
- Distances walked
- The names of your hotels
- The ages of the buildings you visited (very interesting to compare the U.S. versus Europe or Asia on this one!)
- What you ate for breakfast
- Interesting quotations

- New music you heard
- Hours spent traveling
- Miles traveled
- Interesting people you met at restaurants or on trains
- What time you woke up
- Birds you heard
- Your emotions (kids could show this with illustrations or emoticons)
- New foods you tasted
- Interesting words in other languages
- Books you read
- Languages overheard
- Wild animals you saw
- New English vocabulary. By learning new things your kids will inevitably learn new vocabulary, even if the material is not presented in English. For example, they might first hear the word "sarcophagus" at the Egyptian museum or the word "epoch" in a French brochure. A list of English vocabulary can develop into a personal dictionary at the back of the journal. Challenge: your kids could try to use one new word each time they write in their journal.

IN-DEPTH JOURNAL ACTIVITIES

If your child is up for a bigger journaling challenge, the following projects may be fun. These ideas generally take more time and a bit of preparation but they can also be adapted to help you enjoy a fifteen minute break while waiting for the next bus to arrive or the hour you wait on the museum lawn while your spouse and older child are still perusing the museum.

- Use your child as a "camera." Turn his head until it is pointing at a really cool image. Ask him to zoom in or to think about the landscape perspective. Then, have him draw the "photograph" he took in his journal.
- When visiting a park or natural area, create a "nature study." Make a small frame from a blank piece of paper by cutting a hole in the center. The hole can be as big as 7 by 7" or as small as 1 by 1". Put the frame on the ground and observe everything inside the frame. Draw it or describe it in words.
- Look for signs of the season. What can you find that lets you know what season it is? You generally need to keep this going for a few hours to find enough interesting clues. Ask you child, "Aside from the weather, how could you tell what season it is?" and, "How are the signs of summer different here versus at home?"
- Write a poem. This takes time and patience, but it doesn't necessarily need to include rhymes. Who doesn't enjoy a haiku? A haiku is a three-line, non-rhym-

ing poem with exactly five syllables, seven syllables, and five syllables in each line. Getting a young kid to sit down and write a poem on demand seems like a waste of valuable travel minutes, but writing a haiku together over a long walk is a great way to make the walk go quickly while being creative. You can jot the good ones down as you walk and then your child can record their favorites in the journal later.

- Imagine and describe a whole day in the life of someone who lives in your destination (current time or historical time). This is most fun over a whole day: eat breakfast and imagine what breakfast was like for a peasant girl who lived four hundred years ago; then imagine the daily chores; then continue on for the rest of the day. This works well during a trip to a historical or open-air museum!

- Make a marketing campaign or magazine advertisement for your destination. How about using a video camera to make a TV commercial?

- Did your child read a story set on-location before or during the trip that was particularly engrossing? Outline or write a sequel to that story.

- Make up a crossword puzzle using destination-themed vocabulary.

- Discretely watch a person at a café and record every detail: the way they hold their mouth, the line of their clothes, the food that they order, the tone that they use. Add a short story about where that person grew up or about what happened to them earlier that day.

- Pick an interesting word and write about it for ten minutes without stopping. Try "hope," "footsteps," "fame," "curiosity," "art," "legacy," or even "candy."

- Sit at a busy spot, maybe a train station, restaurant, or a bench next to a moving line of people, and write down the bits of conversation that you hear (works best in an English-speaking country). Can you extrapolate the bits of conversation into a story?

ALTERNATIVE IDEAS

If a traditional travel journal isn't your child's style, try one of these alternatives.

Postcard Photo Album

Buy postcards at interesting spots and have your child write on the back of each postcard. She could draw a picture, list her favorite foods at that destination, or describe the best, worst, or most surprising aspects of the place. Slip the postcard into a photo album with both the front and back of the postcard visible or scan and print the writing so that front and back can be displayed side-by-side. At the end of the journey, you'll have an annotated photo book.

Homemade Passport

You can make a "passport" booklet ahead of the trip or create it as you go. Provide one page for each major destination or tourist attraction you plan to visit, list a few questions for reflection, and include an empty square on each page. Use ideas from our journal pages at the end of this chapter. Carry some stickers or tiny

FILL-IN JOURNAL PAGES

It can intimidating to stare at a blank sheet of paper. We sometimes make fill-in pages for our kids to use in journaling. These pages include questions, spots to draw, and bits to record. You might paste in just one page per destination or you might offer a fun fill-in page whenever your child is growing weary or uninspired by journaling.

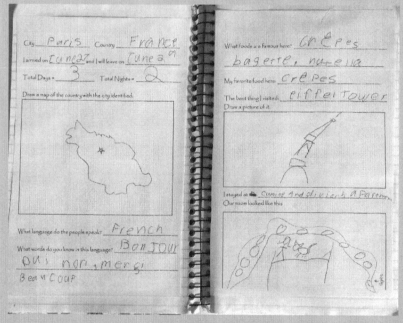

An example of an early fill-in page from Paris.

We provide sample fill-in journal pages at the end of this chapter. Photocopy and paste them into the travel journal or use them as inspiration to create customized fill-in pages that your child might particularly enjoy. Challenge your kids to make fill-in pages for themselves or for each other.

rubber and ink stamps with you. After visiting each destination and filling out the questions, stamp or sticker the empty square.

Sound Journal

Bring along a tiny audio recorder or a small digital video camera and let your kid record sounds. Record throughout the trip or save one or two special days in which you go off listening and recording sounds. Bangkok certainly sounds different from New York City, but what exactly makes the different sounds? Are there announcements on a train that intrigue you? Bird sounds? The calls of street vendors? Some musicians have made symphonies or pop music from street sounds. These would be fun to listen to before the trip if you plan to focus on a sound journal.

Travel Newspaper

At each destination, type a short story or design an advertisement. In the evenings or after you return home, assemble the stories and photos into a short newspaper that tells the story of the trip. "Extra! Extra! Read all about it!"

MEMORIES THAT LAST

The journals we have created on our trips continue to be a wonderful reminder of all of our shared adventures. During the trip, they focus our thoughts about what is different in our travel experiences versus our regular day-to-day lives. Upon our return, they are prominently displayed for easy reference, and often serve to clarify our memories of special travel days. Along with our photo albums and souvenirs, they are long-term reminders of the excitement of experiencing and learning about new things every day. They are also a wonderful way to help ease the transition back home, and keep the spirit of the journey alive for weeks and months to come, as we'll discuss in the next chapter.

TRAVEL JOURNAL PAGES

Use these fill-in journal pages to inspire your kids and add variety to their journaling activities. Many other fill-in pages could be created and customized for your own child.

The first page is intended as a Table of Contents for the beginning of the journal to provide an overview of destinations and dates. Having a Table of Contents may inspire your child to write more frequently so that he can fill in the table. For longer trips, you may want to paste or tape several blank Table of Contents sheets into the front of the journal.

The journal pages are generally ordered so that the first two sheets are more suitable for younger children and the third sheet is better for a slightly older child. However, these pages are designed to be used by a wide range of ages and it's easy to imagine both older and young kids ending up with multiple copies of each worksheet embedded in their travel journal.

Children too young to write or to draw beyond a scribble can work with a parent to answer questions and commission sketches. When parents write down exactly what their children say or sketch what the child remembers, they can provide a nice record of their child's early thoughts and reflections. These notes and drawings can help the child share her trip with friends and family back home (see chapter eight, "Making Memories Stick").

More fill-in pages will become available on our website, familyontheloose.com. If you want to share your own journal pages or ideas, please send them to info@familyontheloose.com.

Travel Journal

Table of Contents

Location	Date	Page

City _____ Country _____

I arrived on _____ and I leave on _____

Total Days: _____ Total Nights: _____

Draw a map of the country and put a star where you are.

What language do people speak here?

_____

What words do you know in this language?

_____

_____

_____

Location _____ Date _____

Best place I went today: _____

Picture of best place:

Best food I ate today: _____

Something funny that happened today:

_____
_____

One thing I learned today:

_____

_____

Other things to remember about today:

_____

_____

_____

Where am I? _____ Date _____

One moment I want to remember:

Quick list: stuff I've done here:

_____
_____
_____
_____
_____
_____

My quick, creative descriptions of life here (adjectives only):

art _____
music _____
fashion _____
transportation _____
architecture _____
history _____
people _____
food _____

Food I've eaten here and my review:
☻ yummy ☺ good ☺ OK ☹ bad ☹ icky

Example: _duck feet_ _____ ⊗

_____ ○
_____ ○
_____ ○
_____ ○
_____ ○
_____ ○

Doodle inspired by my day:

One major way this place is different from home:

_____
_____
_____
_____

One major way this place is the same as home:

_____
_____
_____
_____

Part 3
Traveling Home

Traveling Home

There is nothing like returning to a place that remains unchanged
to find the ways in which you yourself have altered.
　　　　　　　　　　　　　　　　　　　　—Nelson Mandela

You got ready. You got set. You went. You and your kids learned a tremendous amount and every day was an adventure. Now, after all the fun and excitement, you're back home. Reentering your world of carpools, chores, work, and the news in English can be challenging. But your home doesn't have to be the same place you left, and you don't have to be the same people you were when you set out. This section of the book is about how to come back to a "traveling home," and how to hold on to your traveling spirit.

Chapter eight focuses on the trip you've just taken. What ideas did you get *en route* for changing the way you live at home? What reflections and insights can you continue to add to your trip journal? You might even want to structure follow-up activities to compare and contrast your own house, neighborhood, or culture with the ones you've visited. We also provide ideas and advice for remembering, sharing, and enjoying your adventures with your family and friends.

Chapter nine is packed with schemes for home-based travel through day-long excursions and overnight mini-trips. Try out these suggestions between big adventures to enjoy some of what travel offers without having to journey too far—delicious food, fascinating people, and cultural awareness. We list ideas for finding cultural experiences near your own home, for linking multiple activities to explore a particular culture in more depth, and for filling your traveling home with travel-centric toys and books. We hope that these last chapters inspire you to help your kids maintain the open-mindedness and inquisitive attitude that you all share as a family on the loose.

8 Making Memories Stick

You're home! After all that itinerary development, reservation making, packing, and finally getting on the plane, you and your children have now been there and done that. You may be surprised at how quickly you are all reabsorbed into your home life, forgetting the rich details that made the trip a wonderful and potentially life-changing experience.

But the journey is far from over. The memories and spirit of exploration can extend the adventure for months, if not years. By sharing your travel stories, you can re-live and reinforce what you learned on the road. We offer ideas for how your kids (and you) can share their experiences and enthusiasm with extended family, friends, and classmates. The interest of friends will not only solidify the cultural experience your children just had, but will also help your kids keep their enthusiasm for travel and cross-cultural exchange alive and thriving.

Brace Yourself for Reentry Shock

Even when you travel for just a weekend, it's a shock to get back home. The luggage is filled with dirty laundry, there's no milk in the fridge, your e-mail inbox is full, everyone's exhausted, and the adventure seems over. The trip relaxed and recharged you, but the minute you walk back through your front door, the world of responsibility smacks you across the face. After all the planning and anticipation, returning home might even be sad. Being overwhelmed by chores and errands while suffering from post-trip letdown can be a killer combination. We call it "reentry shock."

Overwhelmed parents can get grumpy, and reentry shock absolutely affects your kids too. After six months in Austria, our then fourth grader came home from school and said, "I don't get it Mom. I just wake up, go to school, come home, and then I wake up again. What's the point?" Later, in middle school, it was hard for our pre-teen to discover that even though missed homework didn't have to be turned in post-trip, the material still had to be learned. Her reaction: "Seriously?" Your kids' friends will be ecstatic to see them for about five minutes, but then it's back to life as usual. None of them can really understand the exciting experience that is still so fresh in your child's mind.

Over years of travel, we've come up with a few ideas for minimizing reentry shock:

- Plan a travel dinner with close friends for soon after you return home. Share your photos, eat food from wherever you've been, and let your kids share their journals and souvenirs.
- Schedule one empty day for every week you were away (up to about a week total) for recovery. Don't imagine that you can fly in at 11:30 p.m., clear customs, take a taxi home, unpack the essentials, and get to school or work first thing the next morning.
- Tackle the reentry chores so they don't linger. Before you call anyone, take a few hours to get yourself and the family sorted out: unpack all the suitcases in a flurry, throw in a load of laundry, grab the essentials at the grocery store, sort the mail, and delete all the spam from your inbox. There will still be lots to do but it starts to seem manageable after the first layer of chores is cleared away.
- Be stealthy. Tell folks that you're coming home one or two days after you're really flying in. By the time folks start expecting you to be alert or to answer your e-mail, you'll have found clean underwear and have had a full night's sleep.
- Expect the letdown. If you saved for two years to go on a two-month trip across Asia, coming home is going to be pretty anticlimactic. Plan something special a few weeks after you get home: a trip to your favorite restaurant, a weekend at a local B&B, a special at-home family night. The anticipation for this new event reminds the family about what is special about being at home.
- Start planning the next trip. This might seem a bit like chain-smoking but it helps. Don't book plane tickets or make firm commitments, but explore, "What have we learned about the world and where do we want to go next?"

MAKE MEMORIES A PRIORITY

Fast forward about a week. You've unpacked the suitcases and done many loads of laundry. The refrigerator again contains edible food. The mail has been managed, the pets are used to having you back and so, maybe, are your coworkers. Be careful! It is way too easy to move on from the trip, almost as if it never happened.

Your life and friends will absorb you back quickly and your trip can be erased like a sandcastle under the waves of errands, play dates, and deadlines. Remember that you have a camera full of pictures, a journal bursting with postcards, a few knick-knack souvenirs, a couple of t-shirts, and, hopefully, a new or renewed appetite for discovery. An injection of energy will keep the memories alive and in the front of your kids' (and your own) minds.

Don't let your travel pictures and videos rust on the computer hard drive or allow your journal to disappear into the back corner of a bookcase. We unpack the souvenirs with much hoopla and race to get the photos into easily viewable formats. It doesn't need to take long: organize the photos by location, select the best set of pictures, upload a few to a photo website for prints, put the rest of the good ones on a desktop slide show. Maybe make a new screensaver! If you can manage to make a photo book quickly, do it! It's not as if you are ever, really, going to have more time for photo projects "tomorrow." Your kids will appreciate having something tangible and special to share. Keep the travel reminders accessible on the coffee table or windowsill where they can be the focus of conversation and idle browsing. Make a temporary centerpiece of the souvenirs. Use dinnertime to remember fun and obscure details of your adventure. "What was your favorite restaurant on the whole trip?" "Describe one weird thing that happened on a train." "Which of our friends would have been most shocked on the trip and why?"

If your extended family live far away, it's important to get photos, memories, and trip details delivered to them so they can ask the kids questions and help them stay excited. One option is to subscribe to a digital picture frame service such as Ceiva.com through which you can upload pictures that show up on digital frames in the grandparents' homes the next morning. Making a slide show that can be viewed from an e-mail link is cheaper and easier if you think your family will really click the link, or use Facebook, Flicker, and other social media. If we can't manage a photo book fast enough, we sometimes make a quick photo card with a collage of our photos. The kids mail these out to family with their next set of thank you notes or school pictures.

So what do you do with all the travel tchotchkes after you've grown tired of the centerpiece? If you keep the souvenirs out and about, they get lost, broken, and, eventually, they actually need to get dusted. Sooner or later, even treasures need to be put away somewhere. We've designated a special shelf in each of our kids' bedrooms where souvenirs can be displayed behind glass. One of our daughters specializes in miniature replicas of city icons (for example, the Eiffel Tower, the Leaning Tower of Pisa, Amsterdam's Little Mermaid); the other daughter is more eclectic (sometimes choosing small stuffed animals or maps over statues).

It doesn't matter what they collect—anything that helps them remember where they've been is fun. That said, you might want to avoid things that are a big headache to carry home or to store at home. If you do decide to create a display area, make sure it's big enough to support the souvenirs from future trips. Once bitten by the travel—and souvenir—bug, there is no easy cure.

KEEP READING AND WRITING

Being home is no reason for your kids to stop learning and thinking about where they have journeyed. In fact, there's more to explore once they are at home than there was before. The best insights about a different culture often come when you are reflecting on your trip.

What to Read?

Your kids might particularly enjoy reading books set in the places from which you have just returned. Reading stories about those places had an air of education and discovery before you left; reading or rereading books about that location can be comforting and exciting once you are home again. Does the author describe details that you remember? What did the author leave out? What would you or your kids have added? Would someone who had never been to that location be able to picture it properly from reading the story? Movies set on location, documentaries, travel shows, and historical films about your recent destination can also be more fun than you might expect after you get home. We found about a zillion Alaskan wildlife films and tried to watch them before our trip north but everyone found the films deadly dull. Not surprisingly, as soon as we got home from Alaska, we all wanted to watch them and found them much more interesting and fun.

What to Write?

If your kids found putting together a journal fun and rewarding, they can continue to journal about trip memories and their reentry experience. Did they have any reentry shock? How did the trip change their perspective on their hometown or their own country? What seems different to them now?

Another great angle is to encourage them to start journaling about their hometown. After going somewhere new, your kids may be able to better see what is unique and special about their own backyard (see "Write a Neighborhood Travel Guide"). What would be surprising to a first-time visitor? What really stands out? Are there unique words specific to the area or special foods associated with it? Journaling about home can be really fun and can help your kids notice the unique and special aspects of home that we all, over time, tend to take for granted. Journaling might also be an efficient solution for writing a, "What I Did Last Summer" essay or other school assignment.

If journaling has gotten a bit dull, what about writing a fictional story set "on location" in one of your recent travel destinations? The story could take place during historical times or capture the modern day intrigue of daily life. After a

WRITE A NEIGHBORHOOD TRAVEL GUIDE

Now that you've been a stranger in a strange land, dependent on a travel guide to find the local highlights, why not turn the tables and have your kids make their own travel guide for your hometown or neighborhood?

For younger kids, a guide to the block might be a suitable challenge. Start by making a map and draw arrows to highlight what a stranger might need to know about the place. What would a person from Timbuktu, Paris, or even Omaha want to see on our block? What's special? What's unique? What might take some explaining? Are there visual hints about local holidays or festivals that maybe could be interesting (We bet someone on your block leaves their Christmas lights up all year long)? Any dangers? Are there great trees for climbing? Friendly dogs?

Older kids can make a map of a larger area and point out favorite stores, restaurants, and shortcuts. What should you order at each restaurant? Would the neighborhood travel guide be different for people visiting from different regions, say Asians versus Europeans? What would people from wherever you just visited really need to know? What would they miss from home and want to find in your town? If your young traveler gets engaged in this project, expand it to cover the whole the city. Make some hand-drawn maps, describe the top ten places to visit, and offer some tips. Then bind a copy of this personalized city guide for your guest room nightstand.

Interested in more ideas for writing about your hometown or developing your child's inner travel writer? Look over some restaurant reviews in guidebooks, online, and in the newspaper. Then help your writer visit and review several restaurants near your home. Kids can estimate cost ($ or $$$), describe the service, and comment on the variety on the menu. They can recommend particular dishes. Encourage them to ask the waiter for the house specialty and a list of the most popular items to include in their review. If family members order these likely-to-be-most-delicious items, your junior reviewer might be able to taste a sample for their report as well.

visit to Salem, Massachusetts (famous for witches, hauntings, and hangings) for example, our girls both started writing a whole new genre of literature. Your child's story could be written so that readers have to guess the location. What are the key clues that would tell a reader where the stories take place? What other countries or locations might be easily confused with the true setting? How would the reader know, instantly, that the story isn't set in your hometown?

FOSTER PEN PALS

Keep the trip fresh by fostering and maintaining the personal connections you made during your travels. Maybe you met a kid who would make a great pen pal? Pen pal relationships can still be maintained by old-fashioned snail mail. When else will your kids ever learn to write a letter? For more instant gratification, use e-mail, Skype, and Facebook. Our kids may be growing up taking the internet for granted, but it is still somewhat enchanting to send an electronic note to Hungary at bedtime and to have a reply by morning. Or what about purchasing postcards from your hometown to send to friends you met while traveling? What would be most interesting to them? What daily life details would you write about in that very small space on the postcard? Writing about life back at home helps your kids both reflect and stay in touch.

During longer trips or study abroad exchanges, you may have made real friendships that you deeply want to maintain. Sending information about home might encourage new friends to come visit you or maybe it just helps them visualize your life a little better. Little photo books can be very cheap to create, make a wonderful gift, and are a neat reminder to your kids that they also have a culture and valued traditions to share. Making a small photo book or a personal website documenting "Life Back in America" can illustrate what your child's culture is like at home to their international friends. Sending the photo book or web link also reminds new friends that the friendship is still valuable, maybe even more valuable, now that you are miles apart.

ENGAGE YOUR (KIDS') FRIENDS

You and your kids may be a little taken aback with how little attention even your best friends pay to the travel experience that you've just had. It may have been a life-altering experience for you, but to your friends you might as well have been home sick in bed. "How was your trip? Oh, great! Want to play?" There's a reason why holiday photos are most interesting to those that took the holiday. But whether it's in school or at home, there are a few good ways of getting your kids' friends to pay attention—and we're not above bribery here!

The first incentive perfected through years of birthday party goody bags and trick-or-treating is candy! If you've planned ahead, you can entice a young audience to pay closer attention in exchange for sweets (or trinkets) obtained from wherever you have just been. A class presentation is an opportunity for everyone. A few slides (not too many), a little show and tell, some Q&A, and a sample of foreign sugar can be a lot of educational fun. Candy is usually cheap, easy to carry, and often unique to wherever you've been. Picking out the candy is fun too. There is some weird candy out there! One of our favorites is "Salsagheti" from Mexico: watermelon-flavored hot candy strips with tamarind flavored sauce. Yick! But fun! It doesn't really matter if the kids at home don't like the taste. It's just neat to find out what other kids eat and to dream about the infinite variety of candy that the big, wide world can offer. If you or your kids are really brave and you went some place exotic, you might even consider offering to give a presentation at the local library. Older kids will get great speaking experience and, since the audience is purely voluntary, there will likely be a lot of positive feedback.

How about a destination party? Plan a traditional meal and invite some of your kids' friends (and families) over to try it out. Decorate with flags and photos. Is there a traditional way to set the table? If you are a cooking wimp, feel free to splurge for take out. Have a slideshow (set the slides on auto advance to keep the pace moving along). It's nice to have a map available for reference and perhaps to highlight your route. Maybe play a game from the destination country? If you brought back a game and you can figure out the directions, perfect. If not, you can probably find something online. Movies are always fun (and the kids can eat the souvenir candy while they watch). Cartoons or a kid show from your destination might be hard to find back home, so keep an eye out while traveling. If you're planning to invite adults, by all means, bring home strange liquor to sample and enjoy. Beer or wine produced in your destination are good too. They are hard to carry home but might be available at a large grocery store or wine shop near you.

REACH OUT TO FOREIGNERS

Depending on where you've been, there may also be opportunities to connect to, or even help, folks from your destination who moved close to your home. If you've been to Thailand, go out to eat Thai food and practice your Thai language skills. Is there a local Thai community? A temple? There may be community centers or refugee shelters targeted to specific groups of immigrants near your home and a visit or a donation can be rewarding for everyone. If you've visited a more affluent culture, there are likely to be opportunities back home for connecting through cultural organizations, film previews, and language classes.

HOME SWEET HOME

Post-trip letdown is a natural part of the aftermath of an adventure well taken. But extending the travel spirit into the days and weeks at home following your trip reinforces the memories and learning from your journey. In the next chapter, we'll take this a step further, exploring ways to incorporate cross-cultural adventures into your everyday life and to help your family stay connected to favorite cultures, or get introduced to new ones.

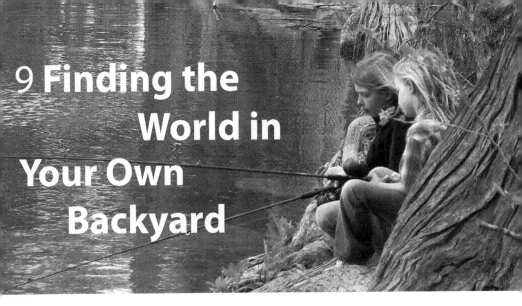

9 Finding the World in Your Own Backyard

W hat is it that makes travel so fun and so educational? Trying new foods? Talking with people who have had different life experiences? Surviving without a toothbrush? Exploring new religious customs? Sights? Sounds? Smells? You can enjoy these experiences between big trips, maybe even in your own neighborhood. In North America, we have a gift that few other places offer: multiculturalism in our own backyard. This chapter is full of ideas for helping your children explore the wealth of cultural diversity that exists near your own home. You may be able to expose them to cultures and ideas from places that are perhaps too far, too expensive, or too unsafe to visit. This chapter isn't about taking a big trip—it's about finding the excitement of tiny trips. The ideas we'll present range from extremely simple (dinner at an ethnic restaurant) to relatively simple (an overnight stay). These easy activities can enrich life and keep your spirit of adventure alive wherever you happen to be.

BE A TOURIST IN YOUR OWN CITY!

It's fun to wake up in a foreign city with a guidebook and a few select adventures on the agenda. You get to walk out the door, forage for breakfast, make plans, trek long distances, ride buses and trains, eat strange foods, stand in museum lines, wander through parks, find authentic restaurants, and find your way back to bed. It's hard to put your finger on exactly what makes it special, but you've learned, enjoyed, bonded, and relaxed all at once. So why not do this at home?

Dig out the guidebook you keep for guests (or invest in an up-to-date guidebook), pick a part of the city you rarely visit (maybe a spot with a cultural theme), and identify something interesting, odd, or touristy to do there. Maybe pick a museum on the other side of town you've never visited, or scan restaurant reviews for something new and quintessential (and maybe not too spendy). Next, figure out the bus or train schedule or look into how you can get around the city by foot (driving and parking are not fun in any city). Set a timeframe and budget and let your kids decide how to spend the hours and money. If you have an infant, plan a little less and schedule your museum visit to coincide with a stroller nap. If you have a pre-teen or teenager, maybe they can invite a friend to explore something independently while you read a book at the coffee shop close by. If you live in a small town, take the bus into the nearest bigger town or big city.

Pack a day bag full of snacks, maps, and colored pencils the night before, get a good night's sleep, and head out. Hopefully, the day will unfold in front of you. There's more time in a day if you reserve it all for wandering, exploring, eating, and enjoying (no errands allowed and—if you dare—turn off your cell phones). Our guess is that you'll be amazed at all the things you've never done in your very own city. Have your kids been to the main icons of town? Have you visited the local history museum? What about the main tourist attraction in the next town over? Just enjoying the relaxed rhythm of a day of family exploration can be a welcome change from play dates, soccer, carpools, chores, and TV.

While you're at it, send postcards! Send them to out-of-town cousins or to friends as encouragement for a visit. Trace your route on a city map. Make a timeline of your own city's history. Create a scavenger hunt of photos (cool views of local icons or funny details that might otherwise be forgotten) that your next out-of-town visitor needs to find when he too spends a day visiting your city. Use the maps, bus schedule, history information, and photo hunt to make a small folder of information, a booklet, or a three-ring binder that lives in your guest room.

Mini-Trips

You may be able to explore a new culture without leaving town. Maybe you're fortunate enough to live near a city with an international district such as the North End in Boston, Chinatown in San Francisco, or Ballard's Scandinavian neighborhood in Seattle? If so, you can easily plan a mini-trip (see "Our Favorite Mini-Trip"). Prepare as you might for any voyage. Get a book from the library, watch a movie, color a map, borrow a language CD, read a fiction story set on location, or try a craft project. Then head over to the international district for a few hours. You can spice up your mini-trip with dinner at an ethnic restaurant or with a stop at an ethnic grocery store on the way home for dinner ingredients.

If you don't live near any exciting cultural centers, you'll have to build your mini-trip from scratch, stringing together activities, arts, and food. You might spend one afternoon on a particular theme or enjoy a month-long theme. The

MINI-TRIP IDEAS

Spice up your mini-trip! Here are some destination-specific ideas for food, special trips, and activities that add flavor and fun.

Africa: Eat Ethiopian food, watch *The Gods Must Be Crazy*, visit a mosque, take a trip to the African Savannah exhibit at your zoo, visit a bead store for African clay beads, make injera, play Mangala.

Australia: Fling a boomerang, make a didgeridoo, watch an episode of Australian television, view aboriginal art and then try dot painting on rocks, visit the kangaroos at the zoo.

Austria: Serve Wiener Schnitzel and try cooking spätzle, watch *The Sound of Music* (though very few Austrians have ever even heard of it), take a waltzing lesson, learn about and listen to Mozart, go for a mountain hike.

Brazil: Read *Magic Treehouse #6: Afternoon on the Amazon,* take a capoeira lesson, slurp a smoothie made with açaí berries, visit the rainforest exhibit at the zoo, make and eat pastels, compare simple phrases in Spanish and Portuguese, visit a Catholic church in a Latin part of town, make a carnival mask, watch *Wasteland* with older kids (or *Rio,* the 3D animated movie).

China: Participate in Chinese New Year celebrations, enjoy dim sum, visit a temple, try kung fu, watch lion dance competitions on YouTube, listen to Chinese folk songs, visit an Asian antiques store.

England: Make tiny sandwiches and serve high tea, buy or make treacle tart, go to a garden, read about Britain's royal history, read Beatrice Potter or *Wind in the Willows*, research King Arthur and the Knights of the Round Table, compare the vocabularies of British and American English, listen to the Beatles, watch *Angelina Ballerina* with younger kids or Harry Potter movies with older ones.

France: Make crêpes, visit the impressionist paintings at your local art museum and try creating your own masterpiece, borrow a French language CD from the library, listen to current French pop music, read *The Little Prince* or *Tintin* (technically written by a Belgian), watch a French clown or mime show, enjoy a baguette with brie and grapes.

Japan: Watch age-appropriate films by director and animator Hayao Miyazaki, try a sushi dinner, do Sudoku puzzles or origami crafts, make sukiyaki at home, visit a bonsai display, take a flower arrangement or karate class, check out anime books, visit a temple.

Mexico: Try traditional Mexican dancing, make and freeze burritos for school lunches, visit a small Latin grocery store, participate in Day of the Dead celebrations and crafts, make a Mayan codex (folded paper book), play traditional Mexican children's games.

Native America: Go to a powwow, try cooking frybread or wild salmon, create paintings from dyes made from native plants, build a miniature birch bark canoe, visit a reservation or Native American cultural center in your local area.

OUR FAVORITE MINI-TRIP: AN OVERNIGHT TRIP TO "CHINA"

Richmond, B.C., a suburb of Vancouver, is more than just another Chinatown. Rumor has it that Richmond's Golden Village, a mere twenty-five miles above the U.S./Canadian border, boasts the largest concentration of Chinese outside of China. It's such a large concentration of Chinese that it can feel pretty much like China itself.

On our first trip, we arrived late and wandered into a mall to find food. No one spoke a word of English. It was as if our two-and-a-half hour car drive had been a fifteen-hour plane flight. We ordered by pointing, smiling, and accepting whatever was offered with appreciation. An older man sat in a grimy chair at the corner of the mall. He had few teeth and a great smile and he watched us approvingly, a little lost family who had tunneled through the Earth only to discover some very yummy fast food. He gave us a lot of nods and several thumbs-up. Now, we try to go to "China" at least once a year.

The kids' favorite stop is the two-story Daiso Store, the dollar store of Japan, not really "China," but a lot of fun. Everything in the store is 100 Yen in Japan, $1.50 in the U.S., and $2 in Canada. And everything includes, well, everything. Erasers, dog toys, stationary, nail polish, plastic storage boxes, belts, plates, tools, toys, bath accessories, exotic candy, school supplies, polka-dotted bags, fuzzy toe socks, green rabbit kitchen timers, yellow plastic banana holders, and dried flowers that had to be designed by Dr. Seuss himself crowd the store.

If you ever manage to extricate yourself from Daiso, you can enjoy the rest of the malls. The Aberdeen Center, for example, has stores you have likely never seen before: a store selling every accessory for your car; a store selling every kind of rice cooker; and a booth selling hundreds of styles of voodoo dolls. The Cube Inc. store is a modern, high-tech consignment store. Something to sell? Rent a clear acrylic cube, decorate it to attract attention, price and display your items. If someone wants to buy from your cube, the store employee will open it and sell the item for you.

There is also a fountain in the middle of the mall that periodically puts on an exuberant water show, orchestrated to piped-in music. The best place to watch the fountain is from the third floor food court (speaking of which, how many types of Asian food are available in the food court? Too many to count!). There are also restaurants, clothing stores, and stores full of plastic food or miniature plastic food (that's two separate stores). Commercial stores within the large indoor malls are fun; wandering aimlessly amid the outdoor strip malls can be a thrill too. We find the billboards strangely pleasing—Chinese characters intermixed with funny English out-of-place phrases such as "Happy Feet" or "Big Bargain." In one strip mall, Ashley wandered over to explore what she thought was a dim sum restaurant and discovered that it was an outlet of sorts, packed with freezers full of dumplings. The variety of creatures in a Chinese pet store, particularly the fish, is worth checking out.

We always plan a visit to a supermarket when we're in the Golden Village (see the section "Have a Grocery Store Adventure"). Wandering the aisles can be an educational adventure unto itself. In 2012, we found a Quaker Instant Oatmeal product in "wolfberry and white fungus" flavor as well as instant coconut gelatin and fresh, imported longans.

The finale of any well-planned trip to Richmond, B.C., should be a dim sum brunch. We've enjoyed inside-out egg rolls, albacore sticky rice, and "mushroom pie" (there was no translation). Sadly, we were already too full to try the assorted shapes of bright yellow Jell-O with red peanuts inside or the brown spongy star-shaped cakes. We ate dim sum once just after the Chinese New Year, and we were treated to a lion dance spectacle that should bring us good luck for several years.

basic elements can be simple: a nonfiction book, a map, a film, a store, and food. If you can toss in a religious center, art exhibit, or other special destination, that's a bonus. You might add an art class, cooking class, or trial language lesson to the mix. The suggestions in "Mini-Trip Ideas" are a great jumping off point.

When picking a culture to study, don't forget our very own North American cultures such as Native Americans from across the lower forty-eight states, First Peoples from across Canada, and Native Alaskans. There is also Cajun culture in Louisiana, Cuban culture in Miami, the Mennonite and Amish cultures of Pennsylvania, Tejano culture in Texas, and the indigenous Polynesian cultures of the Hawaiian Islands.

HAVE A GROCERY STORE ADVENTURE

Food is often the essence of a culture, so sometimes it's wise to lead with your stomach. The most authentic, the best variety, and sometimes even the cheapest international food can be found at specialty grocery stores. You can take a trip half-way around the world at an Asian market, a Mexican convenience store, or a European deli near your home. If you're feeling ambitious, shop for a whole meal. Make a list of ingredients that you need and set out on a quest for straw mushrooms, halva, or instant spätzle.

DESSERT FROM AROUND THE WORLD

In our family we have a New Year's tradition called "Dessert from Around the World." We used to think our kids liked it because it was from around the world but now we think they really like it because it's a whole bunch of dessert. It doesn't really matter though. They love our tradition and its symbolism. Toward the beginning of December, we start scouring the grocery aisles and specialty stores for dessert items that were made in other countries. We're not interested in Italian-style cheesecake or a recipe for Brazilian almond cookies. No, we're talking about items that are made in another country. Chocolate actually made in Germany, Pocky sticks imported from Japan, and candy imported directly from Mexico. There can be some wacky things too, like cake puffs with fish paste inside, sesame seed bars, strange-flavored gummies, or neon yellow cakes. We get a big platter (maybe even two or three) and lay the items out with a small handmade label identifying the country of origin. At dessert time, we each take small samples of everything—in the name of world peace. As these desserts mix together in our stomachs, the very center of this strange orbit of imports and exotic foods, we feel that our kids become citizens of the world. If all these sweets can mingle peacefully in one tummy, then there is hope for world peace as well. Please note that this fancy, symbolic, meaningful, and exciting holiday dessert requires absolutely zero cooking—a big, big bonus!

Not much for cooking? Construct a simple market scavenger hunt, like finding ten items from the sea, six items you've never seen before, or foods from a dozen different countries of origin (read the labels closely). If you're more interested in a quick adventure, simply wander the aisles spotting unusual items. If you are investigating a particular country, look for items from that region or things you've seen people eating in movies. Maybe you've read that the Japanese love Hello Kitty. Can you find Hello Kitty marshmallows stuffed with strawberry jam?

Our favorite aisles include the meat and seafood aisles where there are often live fish, unusual meats, and parts of animals absent in traditional American grocery stores; the fruit and vegetables aisle for healthy alternatives and a taste of the climate (are there tropical fruits or winter greens?); and, of course, the dessert and snacks aisle. Offer your kids a budget. Ten dollars can go a long way toward cultural exploration and understanding at a grocery store. You can also buy a big bag of something to share with friends during school lunch time and spread cultural awareness.

LEARN ABOUT A NEW WAY TO PRAY

Culture and religion have intertwined since the beginning of humanity. While many aspects of culture may be lost during immigration, religion often makes it through. Immigrant communities build temples, mosques, or churches where music, philosophy, literature, and tradition abound. These are treasure troves of cultural discovery!

Ask your kids to estimate how many different religious services take place in your hometown in a given week. Visit some! Often religious centers greet visitors with tours and leaflets. Attend a Baptist church service full of gospel music or maybe participate in a silent Quaker meeting. Take a meditation class at a temple. You can visit most religious centers between services to simply look around. Other religious centers, such as many mosques, ask that you come on a guided tour. Many temples or meditation centers begin in rented houses. We even have friends whose church meets on a basketball court at the Boys and Girls Club because they are too new to have a building. Surf the internet to discover what new religious organizations are meeting near your house. You don't have to adopt the philosophy to visit, but you do have to be open-minded and respectful in other peoples' place of worship.

What will your kids learn about multiculturalism by visiting religious centers? Just the history of the world. You could try to attend a different service every month for a year and compare the experiences. Are there fundamental similarities across all religions? What are they? What are the differences? How are these similarities and differences reflected in the art or the music? What do the religious beliefs reveal about the history of each culture the religion comes from? Has religion shaped culture across different continents or has culture shaped religion? See if older kids can put religious beliefs in the context of current politics. *One World, Many Religions,* by Mary Pope Osborne, is a terrific book that gives a summary of the seven largest religions on Earth and can give your kids background information for thinking about these kinds of questions. You can also read about the history of religion and try to attend services in the chronological order in which religions were born. *The Story of Religion,* by Betsy and Giulio Maestro, is a good place for both kids and adults to begin to learn how and why religions developed.

CELEBRATE SOMETHING NEW!

The cultural diversity in your back yard throws a lot of parties. Attend them all: Chinese New Year, Day of the Dead, Tibetan Culture Night, whatever you can find. Some of these cultural festivals are aimed at insiders, but typically, respectful and interested guests are welcomed. If in doubt, call or e-mail in advance.

Just as you might prepare your kids for a two-week trip to Thailand, prepare them for a two-hour celebration. What are the roots of the ceremony? What symbolic events should you anticipate and what do they mean? We were pretty surprised to learn, for example, that bringing food for the monks at Songkran, is only symbolic. We had worked hard to prepare something they might enjoy; apparently, so had hundreds of other attendees. While we all stood patiently in line to serve them, an industrious group of young men ran along behind the monks, emptying the monk's rice bowls and trays of food into large garbage bags and hauling it away. It would have been better to know in advance that the offering was only symbolic.

You can discover nearby cultural festivals by checking the schedules for local community centers or event halls that often host such events. One weekend there might be a Brazilian festival with dancing, food, and performing arts. A few weeks later, the Philippine community might host a similar event, but with completely different food, dance, and performances. Check the internet and newspapers, look for signs at churches, markets, or ethnic shops, scan corkboards at local universities or community colleges, and check with friends.

TRAVEL IN TIME

Looking for a new travel dimension? Why not explore the past through a Renaissance fair. These often include singing, juggling, jousting, blacksmiths, and more. The Renaissance, which spanned the fourteenth to the seventeenth centuries,

TRAVEL-THEMED BIRTHDAY PARTIES

Why have yet another princess or shark party when you can have a fun, unique travel party? Get your kids excited about a trip you're about to take, share a trip you've recently taken, or enjoy a virtual trip that's not likely to be in your budget for a while.

Ideas for Destination Parties

China: Take the bus to Chinatown or your local international food district, make dragon kites and try to fly them, decorate in red and gold, prepare or eat Chinese food, watch an age-appropriate movie set in China (preferably something more authentic than *Mulan*).

India: Apply henna tattoos, watch a Bollywood film, listen to Indian music, take a yoga class, learn to play cricket, cook and eat Indian food.

France: How about a make your own crêpe bar? You can also serve croissants, French pastries, and quiche. View a slide show of famous French places and famous art (from your own trip or from internet photos). Sketch portraits of each other using big easels (*à la* the artists of Montmartre). Encourage the guests to dress in French clothing and perhaps even give away berets or polka dot scarves as goody-gifts. Have the kids wear them for the meal. French film pour les enfants? *Mais oui! Le Ballon Rouge* (The Red Balloon) is beautiful. Harder-to-find PG-rated French films include *Argent de Poche* (Small Change) or *Va Savoir* (Who Knows?).

Mexico: Listen to Mariachi music, eat Mexican food, watch a movie in Spanish, and, of course, smash a piñata. If you can find a place that makes *tres leches* cake near you, get as much as you can! Also check local Mexican shops (often just tiny shops where you can buy phone cards and send money) for Mexican candy and comic books. Many of these shops also serve bakery-delivered Mexican breakfast pastries. They look cool—so many colors—but they taste pretty unusual. Does your neighborhood have a taco truck?

What about a state-themed party? Alaska with wild salmon, Iditarod dog races, and northern lights? Wisconsin with cheese making, ice fishing, and the Green Bay Packers? Louisiana with crawfish, Mardi Gras, and Zydeco music? Be careful of thoughtless stereotyping, but there are countless ideas here.

offers plenty of exciting education possibilities. Start with nonfiction books on the period, and also on Leonardo DaVinci, Florence, Italy, and the scientific method.

Make a Renaissance week out of it. You could try cooking big turkey legs and serving them on a huge platter with grapes and frosty mugs of old-fashioned soda pop. Or you could venture into some more authentic medieval recipes such as cormarye (roast pork) and pottage of turnips. Watch movies such as *Camelot* (the film version of the musical), *Prince of Foxes* (Orson Wells), or *Don Giovanni* (the film version of Mozart's opera). To embrace the artistic rebirth of the era, paint sketch, and sculpt all week. Perhaps take a real drawing class or pick up a few special supplies such as a little wooden model of a human or an old-fashioned sketch book. Visit a park and paint or sketch. Create a gallery! Make scientific drawings of leaves, plants, or machines. For bedtime stories to read aloud (or for older kids to read alone), try *The Smile* by Donna Jo Napoli (grades 6 to 10) or *The Flying Bed* by Nancy Willard and John Thompson (grades 2 to 4). *Monday with a Mad Genius* is the Magic Treehouse version of time travel to Renaissance-era Italy.

For more travel in time ideas, read the Good Times Travel Agency series about a magical agency that actually offers time travel. Visit ancient Egypt, ancient Greece, the Middle Ages, and other eras past through historical fiction, while learning facts in the nonfiction "travel guide" section of each book. Also check out the Society for Creative Anachronism, dedicated to recreating the world of pre-seventeenth century Europe. They host wars, conferences, and other events. Many groups also recreate the times of the civil war. For example, the American Civil War Museum exhibits living encampments of the Battle of Gettysburg all over the country. You might also find living museums near you or near your next vacation destination. And there are a huge number of small towns famous for maintaining a slice of history such as Tombstone, AZ, (site of the gunfight at the O.K. Corral) or Colonial Williamsburg outside of Washington, DC. Check out ghost towns too! If you become truly committed to traveling in time, apply for a stay at the Danish Land of Legends Museum where you can live for a week as a family in the Stone Age, the Iron Age, or the Viking Age—three generations preferred!

GO TO A CROSS-CULTURAL SUMMER CAMP

You can send your kids to camp in another country or, for a lot less money and hassle, you can send your kids to culture camps near your home. Does the Japanese immersion program have a summer school? Are there camps for Spanish-speaking kids nearby? Check with local language immersion programs that serve students about the same age as your kids. Also check with organizations like the French-American Club or the Philippine Scouts Heritage Society. Cross-cultural camps can be an efficient way to include your family on a work-related trip. While a parent works in a foreign city or even in a nearby town, the kids might have an opportunity to enroll in a cultural camp that doesn't exist at home.

CREATE A CROSS-CULTURAL HOME

Fill your home with cross-cultural resources. Subscribe to kid magazines about travel, about other cultures, or in other languages (if your child is interested in learning another language). You can play travel board games such as *10 Days in Europe* or *10 Days in Asia* that familiarize your child (and you) with geography while enjoying family time. Music from every corner of the planet is available to your family. Listen online to radio stations from around the world or collect music CDs to dovetail with recent trips, upcoming trips, or local expeditions. Of course, fiction and nonfiction books can give you a window into another place or another time. There are also TV shows from around the world online and you can easily rent movies in almost any language and from almost any country. You may need to invest in a multi-region DVD player to play foreign DVDs, but they are now fairly inexpensive and easy to install. A neat resource for developing a cross-cultural home is an e-book called *Bringing the World Home* by Dr. Jessica Voigts at WanderEducators.com. It's packed full of specific suggestions for movies, toys, games, music, magazines, books, TV shows, and more.

INVITE A CULTURE INTO YOUR HOME!

What's the mirror image of a trip around the world? Hosting guests from around the world in your own home. You can experience the trip from the other side. International guests teach you about their culture and also about your own. They expand your way of thinking, help you learn a language, introduce you to new foods, and become lifelong friends. Sure, hosting takes time and some money, but as a host, your kids stay in school and you can keep your job. You don't have to buy plane tickets, deal with jetlag (at least your own), or book hotel rooms.

We've hosted about a dozen foreign students in various capacities and when they leave, we suffer similar letdown to arriving home from the airport after an exciting trip. What makes hosting so fun? "Regular" routines at home become interesting when you can see them through new eyes. For example, having an international visitor paw through the Halloween decorations with you makes them exciting again. Trying on wigs, building a graveyard in the front yard, and explaining the secrets of trick-or-treating reminds you what you like about this holiday but have taken for granted. Guests give you insights too. We asked a European visitor what he thought was most different between Europe and America.

His reply? "Here you don't build your buildings or your infrastructure to last." So true. We think of Europe as having a vast history but we hadn't considered how Europeans might perceive North American history.

You can discover some funny things when you host someone from another country. For example, you might learn about what different people eat in the morning. One of our guests explained to our kids that they should eat candy for breakfast. Why? "It gives you energy for the whole day and doesn't keep you up at night." This same guest also put cold cereal into the microwave. Talk about a new perspective. A young man from Columbia made us scrambled eggs with shavings of ham and peppers accompanied by rich hot chocolate for breakfast. We couldn't have eaten better had we been dining in downtown Tunja.

Shopping in another country is fun. Shopping at home with someone from another country is, again, the inside-out version of that same experience. Bargain juice on sale—four gallons for five bucks—made one of our guests exuberant. What do blue jeans, Nike sweat pants, and Nerds (the candy) have in common? They're all a lot more fun and interesting when you are behind-the-scenes of someone else's trip. Hosting foreign guests can give you an appreciation of how others might see you when you travel too. What do the natives think of us when we are apparently enthralled by the local market or the clothes hanging to dry on a line? A hosting experience helps your kids gain self-awareness, both of how other countries perceive Americans and of what makes us unique as a nationality.

An international family can last a lifetime. Given holiday cards and the ease of internet communication, the relationship can be maintained forever. Ashley still refers to the couple she lived with in Denmark in 1986 as her "Danish parents," which must mean that we now have "children" on four continents. Cultural exchanges link the world together in fascinating and unpredictable ways.

There are a few downsides to hosting people in your home to be honest about. Just as you have to get used to people doing things in new ways when you are "on the loose," you have to get used to guests doing things in new ways right under your own roof. Maybe they don't load the dishwasher the way you would like them to? Maybe the bathroom is filthy or they stay on the internet late at night? Having a relative stranger in your home is not a small thing. But set boundaries, be honest, and don't extend every option until you know them. Make sure you have an option for terminating the home stay if the fit is bad or unsafe.

Hosting costs vary. Although some programs reimburse the host family for meals and incidentals, most opportunities you provide your guest will probably cost you some money—an extra hotel room, another dinner entrée, an extra ticket to the symphony. But there are so many free opportunities to enrich your life and your guest's experience; there's no need to spend a lot of extra money. Remember that many of the most important things you can offer as a host family are the everyday experiences that might seem mundane: grocery shopping, visiting a friend's house for dinner, browsing a craft fair, hiking in the woods, or watching a university sports game. These are difficult experiences to find as a tourist and a big part of what differentiates "living" in another country from "visiting" another country.

A good place to start is with a short home stay or with someone you already know. Do you know an international family with a teenager? Invite him to come visit for a few weeks next summer. Register him for a cool summer camp, plan a fun weekend getaway, and arrange for English lessons. You're off on a "trip" that's cost-effective and educational. All sorts of informal exchanges are possible. There may be international exchanges arranged for visiting orchestras or bands. Sometimes churches and other religious organizations bring visitors to the U.S. You might also find hosting opportunities through your child's school language program. And check with your local university or college. They often have programs to welcome international students.

NEVER STOP EXPLORING

There are an amazing number of ways to bring cross-cultural education into your home without venturing far at all. Sometimes kids resist these activities because they feel awkward or they don't know how to behave. But a little discomfort is an important part of the experience, just as it is when you're traveling farther afield. Embrace the differences, and encourage your children to do the same. Finding multicultural opportunities near home can enrich your family's appreciation for where you live and can expose you to all the other cultures that are transplanted into your own back yard. Opportunities for global education are everywhere. Keep exploring!

Epilogue
Tenets to Travel By

Y ou've reached the very end of this book. Pointing out the two underlying tenets of our traveling (and parenting) philosophy is long overdue. You can carefully set everyone's expectations, keep an impeccable travel journal, and enrich every waking moment of your family's journey, but without these core philosophies, it may all be for naught.

The first tenet? *No guilt.* That's right, no matter how your travels unfold, you should not worry you missed something or, based on what you know now, wonder what you should have done differently. Guilt and regret enrich nothing. Whatever cultural exposure you have given your kids will be invaluable later in their lives. It adds up even if you don't have a lot of time to do research, prepare fancy worksheets, or bankroll a dream expedition. It would be swell to spend six months trekking the kids across Asia, but that's not a realistic possibility for most of us. Still, maybe you can make it to Chinatown in the nearest city, rent library books and videos about different Asian countries, and eat out at local Chinese restaurants. Or if all you can manage is to rent *Mulan* and pick up some Kung Pao chicken at the local grocery deli, do not despair. Perhaps that glimpse will inspire your child to raise money for a trip to China or initiate a different relationship with a Chinese colleague (who will, hopefully, recommend some alternatives to the Disney perspective on her country). Every multicultural experience you give your children builds their awareness of the diversity of people on Earth. Every positive, guilt-free family adventure demonstrates the possibilities for learning from, enjoying, and respecting different cultures.

The second underlying tenet of our travel philosophy is to *have fun.* The whole process of planning and taking a trip should be enjoyable. Fun goes hand-in-hand with our first tenet, because who can really enjoy themselves while feeling guilty? And we don't mean that it should just be fun for the kids. It should also be fun for the adults. If you are the type of parent who views a vacation as a means to get away from your dull and unpleasant kids then, sadly, you've read all the way to the very end only to discover that this book is not for you. A trip is an opportunity to have new experiences with your children, and discover just how interesting and insightful they can be. The nagging is needed less; the rules are far fewer; the opportunities for independence and thoughtful conversation are endless. Adults and children can be partners, each learning from the other and helping to make the trip an exciting and memorable adventure.

If you take away just one thing from this book, we hope it is that family travel is a manageable and exciting part of your children's education. Prepare your kids so that they know what to expect. Prepare yourself with educational entertainment ideas and a can-do approach. The ups and downs are all part of the process. Even very young kids can have fun and be fun on the loose. Once you're out the door, you offer your children not just a one-time vacation but exposure, insight, and an open-minded attitude that will stay with them for their lifetime. Go!

Acknowledgements

We are indebted to Amanda Elkin for editing this book and making our writing so much better. There are few sentences that didn't benefit from her patience and skill. Leslie Wall spun our ideas and old photos into a gorgeous cover and enriched our content by organizing the inside of the book. Her formatting of all those reproducible pages has given them life. Britt McCombs jumped in at the last minute and, with enthusiasm, gave the book its final polish.

Many friends contributed to our project. We are grateful to Michelle Bemis and Jan Lorey Hood for typo eradication. We thank Dale Thornburgh, Sarah Jacobson, and Jodie Gahard for ideas on how they have traveled either with their kids or with their parents. We thank Eleanor Huston for sharing her fun yet educational math game. Helen Buttemer reminded us to include ecology and offered a small library of idea resources. We are grateful to Tom Short and Anne Tessman for hosting us in Japan and saying "You know, we thought you were crazy but, actually, all that preparation paid off." Leina Johansson edited early versions of our proposal and encouraged us to write less like scientists. We also thank the Austrian-American Educational Commission and the Fulbright Program for enabling us to live in Vienna as a family. And we would particularly like to thank the countless friends who, upon hearing of our book idea said, "that sounds like a book I would buy."

We now also appreciate the endless agents and publishers who gave us the freedom to self-publish. Tarik Abouzied nudged us to see self-publishing as a viable option by helping to design and build our website: "You're closer than you think you are." Jen Grinell, Don Gallager, and Kate Johnson helped us make connections and get started. Jessie Voigts welcomed Ashley to the blogging world and Camille Hubac, who read our posts enthusiastically, successfully tested our ideas with her own family. Caroline Caskey and Gillian SteelFisher sent motivating feedback.

None of this would have happened without our family. Our parents introduced us both at an early age to a respect for other cultures, and brought us on our earliest adventures. Our kids, Zoey and Logan, have been our traveling companions for over a decade and continue to inspire us to see the world in new and challenging ways. They have endured many "book nights" and injected our writing with their kid perspective and insight. We thank and love you all.

About the Authors

Bill Richards and Ashley Steel have traveled to over forty countries and have two wonderful and well-traveled daughters. As a family, they have lived in or visited the United States, Canada, Asia, Eastern Europe, Western Europe, and the United Kingdom. The idea for this book was hatched when they over-prepared for a trip to Japan and discovered that their preparations made the trip particularly successful. The book grew slowly for several years on cocktail napkins and scraps of paper until the first words were finally typed into a computer.

Bill Richards is an accomplished forest ecologist, specializing in restoring forest habitat for rare wildlife species. His work has appeared in the *Natural Areas Journal, Conservation Biology,* and *Forest Ecology and Management.* Bill grew up on both sides of the U.S.-Canadian border and accompanied his parents to over a dozen countries before graduating from high school. He has also lived and worked in Australia, Thailand, and Austria, and has traveled extensively in Central America, Eastern and Western Europe, and West, Southeast, and East Asia.

E. Ashley Steel, Ph.D., is a research scientist specializing in river ecology and statistics. She spent many summers teaching science to kids at a University of Washington academic summer program, leading students on enriching adventures with activity pages and worksheets. She cofounded the Science Inquiry and Research Council (SIRC), a nonprofit organization focused on improving science education. Her published curriculum, *The Truth About Science,* has sold over 5,000 copies. Her academic travel bug was ignited in college during a semester in Denmark, and she has since been honored with a Luce Fellowship for a year in southern Thailand, and a Fulbright Fellowship to live and work in Austria.

Colophon
A note on the type:
Text is set in Minion Pro and Myriad Pro,
an OpenType update of the original families designed by Robert Slimbach,
issued in digital forms by Adobe Systems,
Mountain View, California, in 2000.

Worksheet and cover text is Parade,
issued by URW++,
Hamburg, Germany.

Cover and chapter header photographs were taken by either
Bill Richards or Ashley Steel.

This book was designed by Leslie Wall,
Lumpfish Design,
Seattle, Washington.

Made in the USA
Lexington, KY
20 April 2013